God's Way to be Human

God's Way
to be Human

meditations on following Christ
through scripture and sacrament

GEOFFREY PRESTON O.P.

Posthumous texts prepared, with a memoir,
by Aidan Nichols O.P.

PAULIST PRESS
New York/Ramsey/Toronto

First published in Great Britain as *God's Way to be Man* by Darton, Longman &
Todd, Ltd. Copyright © 1978 by The English Province of the Order of Preach-
ers.

Library of Congress
Catalog Card Number 78-65902

ISBN: 0-8091-0280-3

Published by Paulist Press
Editorial Office: 1865 Broadway, New York, N.Y. 10023
Business Office: 545 Island Road, Ramsey, N.J. 07446

Printed and bound in the
United States of America

Contents

Geoffrey Preston O.P.

Geoffrey Preston was born in his grandmother's house in Winsford, Cheshire, in the February of 1936. Winsford is a typical town of the Cheshire plain, where the low landscape stretches away to the horizon, broken in those pre-war years by the salt-mining works and the clustering villages now commandeered increasingly by Manchester businessmen. Geoffrey's earliest years were spent not at Winsford, however, but at one of these villages, Beeston Castle, where his father was a local blacksmith like his father before him. From the windows of their cottage it was possible to take in both Beeston Castle and Peckforton Castle, and those early images no doubt played their part in his later fascination with history as a discipline. Yet this family background was more consequential than merely suggesting a university course. People spoke, after his death, of his 'peasant simplicity', a curious phrase for such a voraciously intellectual man. He had a sense of first principles and of primary human values, a respect for the local and the particular, a sharpness in picking up the spirit of place, a capacity to put down roots into the human soil of wherever he was and a love for the countryside of a quite unsentimental kind, such that the word 'peasant' in fact suited him down to the ground. It would be hard to place his politics but, at the foundations, he was the best kind of natural conservative. He had the countryman's disbelief in large theoretical schemes of improvement, together with his concern for the underdog and wrath at any hubris on the part of the powerful. He was a little like First Isaiah in this. Only he was very English.

His father's health broke down when Geoffrey was three. The difficulties in the family's circumstances that followed had an enduring significance, not in breeding any sort of resentment or bitterness but in giving him a quick, sympathetic understanding of sickness and poverty. There were two compensating factors in these troubles. The first was the life and devotion of the Methodist church, to which his father's people were deeply and permanently attached. When, years later, Geoffrey became a catholic he entered, as he put it, 'a larger room', yet in one important sense he remained, consciously and proudly, a child of the Wesleyan tradition. To this element in his upbringing belong his sense of the transcendence of God and his feeling for the local congregation as fully the church in its own place, as well as his love for the Bible and his extraordinary inwardness in getting beneath the skin of the scriptual text. The very way he handled the book was remarkable. He said that everyone should have a copy to read and meditate upon and another to study and mark. He loved congregational hymns and took their theological content seriously, though his rendering of them resembled a cow roaring.

The other strongly positive element Geoffrey found in his childhood was a love of learning. He entered grammar school at the start of the post-war era of expansion which brought the best of classical English schooling within the reach of the children of working people. His teenage years were spent in the meritocratic fifties and like many other gifted children of the time he was attracted strongly and unquestioningly to the prizes of success. At Durham University, when he was able to take up his place there to read History after two years of national service with the Royal Air Force, he came to preside over a medley of societies, the Radical Society, the History Society and the Union, and most improbably for a man of his physical proportions, the Tennis Club. Those who knew Geoffrey solely as a friar and a priest have been surprised to learn that he held a university prize for debating, since his intellect became thoroughly receptive and contemplative rather than argumentative. But the common factor which persisted from school to the Dominican Order was a habit of omnivorous reading and a delight in information on matters common and out-of-the-way alike. He liked to populate the world with succulent facts. It was an attitude with nothing of the defensive about it: it stemmed from an exhilaration, perhaps especially Dominican, before all the faces of creation. In his later years his cell was crammed from ceiling to floor with books on every conceivable subject, even though theology was monarch there. Gypsies to dancing, all was grist to Geoffrey's millstones which crushed from what he read every particle that might be of service to faith. He saved up quotations in commonplace books on the Elizabethan model. He never read without a pencil beside him, even in works of fiction. He used to say that, although Dominicans should be theologians and not astronomers-royal, which was safer left to Jesuits, they should have gutted at least one book on astronomy since, after all, God was the God of astronomy as well.*

It was at Durham, while taking a diploma in Education to prepare himself, as he thought, for teaching the young, that Geoffrey set off on the odyssey which took him through Anglicanism to the catholic church and eventually into one of its most venerable religious orders. Humanly speaking, it seems to have been a thirst for spiritual spaciousness that impelled this journey. He wanted to share a room with Donne and Andrewes and Herbert, as later on he would with the Fathers of the Latin West and the Greek East, with Anselm and Bernard and Thomas, and eventually, as his sense of 'masters in Israel' became wider, with Teresa and Ignatius Loyola, Francis de Sales and Cardinal Bérulle. Writers somewhat out of favour in modern roman catholicism he would rescue lovingly from second-hand bookshops in London or the Wye Valley. He came to have an extraordinarily rich and attractive sense of the catholic tradition as a common pool of wisdom and example in the communion of saints. His Anglican time was, however, a brief and not especially significant one in this development. His Nonconformist origins gave him, possibly, a native dislike for religious establishments: something almost palpable when one accompanied him round the more splendid fanes of the 'ecclesia anglicana'. He encountered Anglo-

---

* His collection of books now forms the nucleus of the Geoffrey Preston Library housed in the Catholic Chaplaincy of Leicester University and reflecting his interests and concerns. As well as being of wide use in a University (and Polytechnic) without established teaching faculties in theology, this Library will serve as a permanent memorial to him. Gifts of books may be made to the Chaplains, Holy Cross Priory, Wellington Street Leicester, LE1 6HW, and financial contributions should be made payable to the Leicester Catholic Chaplaincy Association and sent to the Honorary Treasurer, Dr. Michael Le Bas, Department of Geology, The University of Leicester, Leicester, LE1 7RH.

Catholicism in the form of a Marian procession in reparation for televised unchastity, held during Evensong in a West End square in the parish of a well-known London church. It was enough. He had a horror of the demonstrative in religion, though he saw good ritual as avoiding just such inauthentic over-statement. It was perhaps a mercy that he travelled so little in the traditionally catholic parts of Europe. On his becoming a catholic he took a teaching post in a boys' secondary school run by Irish teaching brothers on the Fylde Coast of Lancashire. No spiritual préciosité could survive the meeting with Anglo-Irish and recusant catholicism. By reaction, the experience fed his desire to get as deeply as possible into a living and articulate theological culture which would draw together his sense of God and of human community, his zest for knowledge and a call to communicate to others. To say that he found all this in the Dominican Order would be at once to say too much and too little.

When at Oxford in 1970 he became novice-master in the Order he had entered only nine years before, he liked to commend to his novices Dom Jean Leclerq's book on the monastic culture of the high Middle Ages whose title sums up the two chief strands in Geoffrey's attraction to the English Dominicans, *The Love of Learning and the Desire for God*. This initial monastic and contemplative orientation was, however, something he had to struggle with for the rest of his life. It was lost and re-found. It could not be enjoyed in innocence, for he found aspects of himself, and aspects of the institution he lived in, that were recalcitrant to this, yet somehow had to be integrated. The cost was great. His first years as a religious (the term is used in the technical sense of a person committed to the christian life under some version of the vows of poverty, chastity and obedience) were spent in large and rambling Victorian houses in the countryside of Gloucestershire and Staffordshire. The Dominican life there, largely unchanged since its revival in a slightly self-conscious neo-Gothic form in the nineteenth century, proved unprepared to meet the crisis of the questioning of all assumptions that Pope John XXIII's revolution brought on the roman catholic church in the 1960s. Many felt that only a good dose of secularism and concentration on the pastoral would enable a thirteenth-century religious order to speak to people in a Britian then changing culturally at a breath-taking pace. It would be true to say, one may

10

hazard, that the pattern of aspirations Geoffrey had set himself fell apart at that moment, and that it took him the remainder of his short life to put them together again. The process had so many sides that different people inevitably saw chiefly one or another, although many of those who knew him had a sense of the complexity and unexpectedness of his judgments and passions. It made of him almost, but not quite, a great man.

Geoffrey's personal crisis was in its own way a paradigm of that of the whole church in his lifetime. It involved asking, and asking extremely persistently, the question which has governed christian life, and particularly the life of christian religious, at all turning-points. Where is God to be found? The meditations that follow in this book touch time and again on a dialectic of the absence and the presence of God. Geoffrey was temperamentally a man who trusted human culture, all tried and tested human things. He had nothing of the iconoclast about him. But he saw, in that torturingly difficult decade of the 60s, that to rely on a historical culture, whether wesleyan or catholic or, more specifically, that of the English Dominicans, to bring God to one was a rank kind of superstition. The discovery, given the warmth of his historical attachments, did not fail to hurt him. It drew from him a temporary acerbity against traditional catholic patterns of life and worship in which this enormous, bovine, cheerful, inquisitive and childlike man found it in him to hurt others by what seemed, but was not, a careless radicalism. But as he approached priestly ordination and began his ministry he realised, it seems, that this necessary deflation of an over-confident church-culture was not enough. If the living God were to be found within the common life of his Dominican brethren and among the groups of layfolk he served at Oxford and elsewhere, the clues to his presence could only be uncovered in some rapport with the liturgical, spiritual and theological tradition which linked the church now with the time of Jesus and his disciples, even if this rapport were a good deal more taxing, deep and strenuous in the attaining than he had once thought. This was a desert experience of the classical kind, in which the image of God is broken and re-made in an interior suffering which hardly anyone else can share. From it issued a striking ministry of teaching and preaching and pastoral care. His gifts as a liturgist, a man of ritual, were out of the ordinary. He had a facility for combining the intimate with the solemn which made it thankfully impossible to claim him as either a progressive or a traditionalist. He could not only see but practise the strengths of both parties. He could understand and share the impatience of many with the limitations of the historical catholic church, although he knew there was no other. He could feel for and express the anxieties of catholics dismayed and bewildered by the loss of moorings in the post-conciliar church, although he knew there was no way back to a pre-lapsarian Eden. Most important of all, in his own eventually serene possession of ancient and modern, held together in a personal unity, he gave people a sign that can justly be called, in the over-worked phrase, 'prophetic' for the future of the church of Christ.

It was to contemplative religious and chiefly to the women among them that he gave most in these terms. It has been among them that the sense of his loss, at the age of forty-one, is most acutely voiced. That is, it has been among people for whom theological matters, so far from being synonmous with academic irrelevance to life, are the very stuff of existence, since the life of believing simply is their life. Two things stand out, in considering the comments they have made.* One is the relief which his theological and spiritual balance brought, his lack of either hasty and negative fashionable critisms or that embattled defensiveness which betrays its own secret loss of confidence. There was a wholeness in his presentation of the christian life, and of the great mysteries of God, Christ and the church. The other is the degree of personal appropriation he had made, in his own heart and mind, of the teaching he gave. Controversial and controverted as his views might be on a variety of topics, when he spoke of Scripture, according to one enclosed Carmelite, 'one could only feel that here was a man speaking of what he knew, and what he knew not "through flesh and blood or through the will of man"[1] but through the grace of the Father. There may well be others who have a greater technical knowledge of God's Word, but none who could so hold it up to his hearers in all its divine radiance. For this, his loss is irreparable'. It is often the case that people who exercise spiritual fatherhood in communicating the life of the spirit to others carry the distinctive cross of finding no-one

* I am grateful to such religious and to many others who have offered impressions of Geoffrey used in the making of this personal sketch.

themselves in whom to confide. But in Geoffrey's case whatever he gave to such women he received back in occasions of understanding, in which the grace of spiritual motherhood in them bore fruit in a re-possession of self in him. How much he needed this his own Dominican brethen can scarcely say since it was, paradoxically enough, among them that the gains of his desert experience proved most difficult to communicate. There was a hurt in him which had not healed, its symptom an inability to risk opening himself fully to them. Like all such hurts this condition hastened the spread of a dis-ease of the self. To some extent, in his years as novice-master, he lost his sense of self-value. It was only, perhaps, his election as prior of the community of Holy Cross, Leicester, in 1976 that restored this in the presence of his brethren. He would admit frankly to such women the tremendous amount it meant to him to be honoured by the trust of his fellow-Dominicans. They could see how simply and sweetly this human security restored his spiritual confidence. It was right that it should be two friars of the Leicester house, then, who were with him when he collapsed suddenly at Hawksyard Priory, Staffordshire, on the Monday of the first week of Passiontide, 1977. Gall-bladder trouble was diagnosed but the surgeons could not operate immediately because of his size. Three days later the same brethren were called in haste to his bedside. The heart had failed, and they saw his body relax finally in death.

In that last year, when he was prior of Leicester, the strands came together sufficiently to justify looking at this death on the thirty-first of March, 1977, as not so much tragic as the plucking of the ripened fruit. With his brethren in that year he was a pillar of strength, communicating indefinably a sense of the reality of God and of joy in God. With his people he was a memorable pastor, loving everything he did, whether discussions with the university students or receiving an old lady into the church, catechising children or taking communion to the sick, which he did by bicycle at seven in the morning, daily and perilously, for his girth had by now reached Falstaffian dimensions. One person remembers him most characteristically as sitting for hours at the bedside of an elderly sister with verbal diarrhoea who thought, mistakenly, that she was dying and had a grip like the ancient mariner. Another sees him most clearly caught in a conversation with an atheist, where his complete lack of narrowness of mind communicated its own direct and honest sympathy. One of the brethren cannot eradicate the image of that great mass of a man in a slightly grubby cream serge Dominican habit, occupying an armchair with the air of a beached whale, a rosary in his fingers and the Authorised Version of the Bible on his tummy. Someone will remember him for remembering the trivial but telling detail of their own history. A non-catholic in Leicester writes to the local paper how in some personal distress they telephoned and found a man who would sit supportively with them in the solitude of the priory church in the early hours of each morning. A nun in Norway remarks on his immediate appreciation of things and persons, his enjoyment of what was novel and strange in creation as a mirror for the ingenuity of God.

The same woman happened to note how in the intervals of retreat-giving he would clamber off to look at the luxuriant wild flowers of the brief Arctic summer and bring a few gently home. Perhaps that may serve as a final image of him. Such vulnerability, and such godly beauty. Truly, as the apostle Paul says, 'We have this treasure in earthen vessels, to show that the transcendent power belongs to God and not to us'.[2]

Aidan Nichols O.P.

Foreword: Following Christ

What being a christian means can emerge from any number of possible angles. I would like to reflect on two. The christian is a disciple of Jesus of Nazareth, and he is a living and acting member of the church of Christ. Each of us, in one way or another, has answered that call, 'Come, follow me':[3] even if those words do not mean literally, as they did for the first christian generation, 'Go on the road with me'. Equally, each of us, in one way or another, lives within the communion and fellowship of other people who have also heard that call and have done something about answering it. If we are going to meditate on what it means to be a christian, we could do worse than to look at the person whom in one way or another we are following, and at the society of those who are following him with us, through the classic moments and expressions of its life, the sacraments. Our looking at the christian life will mean looking at Jesus of Nazareth in his historical existence, and at Jesus in his existence as church, the whole Christ.

To enter into contact with the historical Jesus we must travel through the founding documents of the church, which share with his person the title Word of God. We can find him in the scriptures, and most particularly in the gospels. There, as in the Bible as a whole, we find an attempt at narration, at telling a story. From the standpoint of christian (and jewish) tradition, the life abundant that faith promises is offered in virtue of a story being told. As in the best narration, a real effort is made to be true to the facts. But the incidents are related not because they happened but because of the significance they had for the people for whom each gospel-writer is speaking. The events are narrated in each a way that the divine meaning which lies in the story of Jesus can appear, for 'res tua agitur', it is your existence which is under discussion here.

For the life of Jesus as church we have a privileged expression in those moments we call sacraments, for in those activities what Jesus means for us men and for our salvation is enacted and played out. The christian church is the gathering of people which occurs when someone starts to tell the story of Jesus as the story of a man from the past who *still* comes and makes ultimate demands on those who hear the story. The church is what happens when the story of Jesus is told. Yet for this to be so the story must be told dramatically; indeed, it insists on being told with rite and gesture. It forces us to tell it sacramentally. 'All that was visible in Christ our Redeemer has passed into the sacraments of the church'.[4] The sacraments are the articulated telling of the story of Jesus of Nazareth, proclaiming the many ways in which he is still present for us, we who have heard the word about him and in some way or another have given a yes to it. The seven of the traditional seven sacraments is primarily the seven of the symbolism of number, the symbol of fulness, rather than the seven of arithmetic, the seven of quantity. The sacraments spell out in their fulness the ways in which Jesus of Nazareth still comes in order to be for us. Where the sacraments are concerned, participating in them comes before thinking about them. We must let ourselves go into the internal rhythms and modalities of the sacramental celebration. Yet this celebration involves thinking, for it involves words. If we are to encounter the Lord Jesus in the sacraments we have to listen to language, since faith depends on hearing, on learning a new language, on being prepared to be taught.

It is only by letting scripture and sacraments and our own human existence interpret each other that we shall follow Jesus with full fidelity and find in him the conversation and meeting of God and man. Let us set off then, that we too may live and die with him.

1

Baptism

The first way in which we are taught what Jesus wants to be
for us in the sacramental life of the church is baptism. In
baptism we become disciples, entering upon the way of following Jesus and beginning to walk the way of the cross after him.
It is a beginning in fulness. We can never get beyond our
baptism: this is why retreats and missions traditionally end
with a renewal of baptismal promises; why the whole church
puts herself back at the font on Easter Night and goes to the
font in procession each day in Easter week; why at the Lord's
own service (the Mass) on the Lord's own day (Sunday) the
Lord's own people (the church) are sprinkled week in, week
out, with the water of the Asperges. Baptism is never simply
over and done with, for it is a persisting element in the christian life. 'We little fish, after the example of our IXTHUS
Jesus Christ, are born in water, nor have we safety in any
other way than by permanently abiding in that water'.[5] We
need time and again to think about what it was we were
playing at when we went under the waters of the font. Most of
us were baptised in our infancy in rather a quiet and
unspetacular way. But if we are thinking about any sacrament
we need to think about it in the fulness of its celebration rather
than in any of the attenuated ways in which it can quite
rightly and properly be celebrated. We shall best understand
what a sacrament is if we let our reflections turn on the sign in
its fulness. We should think of the adult convert from unbelief
or paganism on Easter night, when the Lord's resurrection is
proclaimed. After the long readings the candidate is stripped

naked and, standing in the waters, hears a series of questions fired at him. 'Do you believe in God the Father who made heaven and earth.' 'Do you believe in God the Son who was born and lived and died and rose and was glorified and is coming again?' 'Do you believe in the Holy Spirit who in Holy Church is the forgiveness of sin and the pledge of the resurrection of the flesh?' As the man assents to one chapter after another of the story, so time after time he is seized and thrust under the water, not knowing whether he will come up again or not, not knowing what is happening to him and what will happen. But eventually he does come up again. He is raised up, anointed with sweet oil, clothed in clean garments and led to the bishop, who represents both the gathering as a whole and the Lord of the gathering. The bishop calls down the Holy Spirit upon him so that he may dream dreams and see visions, and finally he is kissed by all his new brethren, who thereby welcome him as God welcomes him. If we are thinking of the significance of our baptism for us now, those are the sort of images to which we need to give free play in our minds and hearts.

Baptism is 'necessary for salvation', at least for those who see that it might be so necessary. That is to say, it is the answer to the question, 'What must I do to be saved?' This is the question posed time and again in the New Testament by those who have heard the Jesus story and been overwhelmed and put under threat by it: what must we do? The answer is the absurd command: Be baptised. Go through that extraordinary business of being stripped of all your pretences, of all the ways in which you present yourself to other people, and be stripped of it all in their presence. Give up your pretences. Be honest: let go, trust, give yourself into their hands. Trust yourself and your future, your life itself to them. Seek no guarantees, but do what they tell you, even such absurd things as stepping down into a bath of water and allowing yourself to be plunged under without any certainty that you will come up again. This is why baptism is par excellence the sacrament of faith, for in this sacrament trusting ourselves to other people in the sense of letting ourselves be seen by them, without their having to listen to what we make of ourselves, is precisely how we are saved. That is how in baptism we come to 'put on'[6] Christ, in that metaphor borrowed once again from clothing. It may be more helpful to think not so much of putting on an overcoat as of putting on weight, for it is the latter that makes such a difference to one's personality. What the metaphors are saying is that we must put off our pretence, put away the history we have known, and take on another. We must give up what we most fundamentally are, let our heart be taken from us and receive a new heart, a new centre of gravity. We have to accept a new spirit, letting our spirit be none other than the Holy Spirit of God who can only be spoken of in terms of wind and flame and water. We have to accept a new name, for faith is a person-making activity, the acceptance of a new context of meaning for our lives, and so indeed a new life for an old.

Any christian way of life is a way of making permanent this search for a new identity, for a new heart and a new soul. The search is always made with other people, those who belong to the new history we have opted for, the hundredfold of brothers God gives us. Our new identity will come as a gift to us in the fellowship of our brethren, but only if we pay the cost of remaining true to the beginning-in-fulness which was our baptism, of continuing to be prepared to trust the brotherhood. The price we pay is our prized capacity to present ourselves to others with a set of pretences, masks and postures; instead, as far as we can we present ourselves as we are. As far as we can, because it is difficult enough to have even self-knowledge, we show ourselves to them as we are. Indeed, our knowledge of ourselves itself only comes to the extent that we are thus prepared to trust ourselves to others. Similarly, by this baptismal candour we create a situation in which other people are able to learn to trust themselves and learn to be honest with us.

In every group somebody has to be prepared to begin again this business of trusting and being trustworthy, even though it carries all the danger of entrusting yourself in the font to another person. It is a playing with fire. In the celebration of baptism on Easter Night the church teaches us to play with fire, to pass on the flame of Christ from one person's candle to the next. Trust is a style of life, a style which rises out of a series of different acts of trusting each other, but which is greater than the sum of all those individual acts. Trust is the air we breathe in the church, the air which we are committed to trying to keep unpolluted or to purifying when it inevitably becomes polluted. Trust, which is only another way of talking about faith, is like that peculiarly christian kind of loving called charity. It is one and the same thing whether it is directed to God or to our brethren. If we do not love our brethren, how can we trust God? How can we have faith in God whom we have not seen if we do not have faith in our brother whom we have seen? And conversely, we are closing the possibility of his trusting God if we are not ourselves the kind of people who can be trusted. In our childhood we were told not to go near the water, nor play with fire. But we have to immerse ourselves in the destructive element and be burned up if we are going to be able to find a new identity, a new self, as we do by choosing God to be our God and these others who are his to be our brothers. We choose these others because they are already chosen by God, who has taken them as they are. They too have let themselves go under in the waters and, like Peter sinking under the waves, have reached out a hand and had their hand grasped by Christ. What matters now is what God makes of them. Our attitude to one another cannot be that of condemning and judging, picking and choosing, deciding whom we will and whom we will not favour. We affirm the catholicity of the new creation in being baptised, and if our christian life is to be a true imaging of the baptismal life it must be genuinely catholic in its acceptance of others. We must beware of that trick of all communities of defining themselves by reference to an outsider. So often we let some person be the long-stop, the 'ne plus ultra', the one who is just beyond the pale, such that the community we belong to knows itself as a community by knowing that it is not like that person. But baptismal life means that we are all in it together. George Fox used to pray 'to be baptised into a sense of all conditions, that I might know the needs and feel the sorrows of all'.[7] In being baptised we are identifying ourselves with the sinful mass of humanity and the 'permixtum corpus' of the catholic church, and that too we never get beyond. We are always dependent on the pure grace of God, altogether unmerited and utterly unexpected.

If we refuse to settle for a situation in which our communities have their outsider in the midst then life becomes more unsettled because more dangerous. The reality of playing around with fire and water is martyrdom, perhaps the long slow martyrdom of witness, but most typically the baptism of blood. The martyr is the type of the church. In looking at the martyr you see the church. Baptism of blood is not a poor substitute for water baptism but the reality, the real dying into the passion of Christ, of which water baptism is an image and a sacrament. Martyrdom, the violent death for the sake of Christ, sums up years and years which in the moment of martyrdom are discovered as ordered to it in advance, a long preparation. That moment (like other typical moments in a man's life – marriage or religious profession perhaps, certainly physical death) makes new sense of the whole succession of moments over the course of the many years which led to it. In baptism the reverse happens: the moment of truth comes first, and in advance relieves the succession of moments that will follow from the necessity of being 'just one damned thing after another', conferring on them instead the possibility of a significance that abides. That is only a possibility, however, for we have to go on affirming our baptism. Each of us is invited to internalise it, and to realise in the strong sense of the word that being once-born will not suffice. We must either pass over or perish. It is in this way that the baptisand is crucified with Christ, risen with Christ, seated in the heavenly places with Christ. It is in this way that he shares a common history and a common destiny with Jesus of Nazareth whom God has made Lord and Christ.

2

The Birth and Infancy of Jesus

The christian, the baptised man, is one who follows Christ; what is involved should emerge, amongst other ways, in meditating on the Lord himself. In such meditation we 'look to Jesus who began our faith and brings it to completion',[8] as the author of the Letter to the Hebrews puts it. We will learn to have that mind in us which was also in Christ Jesus if we allow ourselves to learn what was the mind which was in Christ Jesus. This we do primarily through the scriptures, as acted out in sacramental celebration but also as read and proclaimed. We do not look for the Jesus behind the scriptures, but the Jesus of the scriptures; for the scriptures, and more particularly the gospels, are one of the ways in which Jesus bodies himself forth in the world. That is why the church has recommended to us styles of prayer like the rosary, or the way of the cross in its more ancient form, which consist in a listening to Jesus in the scriptures.

In such forms of prayer, which invite us to worship and thanksgiving in the contemplation of Jesus, the Son of Mary, as the Way to the Father, we look at and listen to the one who is man-for-us and God-for-us, in whom the long story of God's dealings with man comes to its heart and home. In the Bible God begins to speak (using 'speak' in a highly attenuated sense) in cosmic events or in historical happenings, in earthquakes and volcanoes and winds and floods, in the escape of a motley crew of slaves from Egypt, in some people's being allowed to go home from exile in Babylon. The story becomes increasingly human until in the end it is a history of

Immanuel, God-with-us, God living a human life. It ends with the complete humanity of a person of whom it can be said that anybody who sees him sees the Father. It ends with one in whom can be seen the source, ground and significance of all that is, primordial Being, the condition that there should be anything at all; and in this man we can see also that this ground of being and granite of it may be addressed in personal terms as Father. We can now call 'our Father' to the wellspring of nature and the Lord of history. Jesus is the en-manment of God, and in him the world and history are humanised. Jesus, as John Donne would say, contracts the immensities and focusses the infinite. He is God focussed to a point. He is the face of God. In him immensity was cloistered in the dear womb of Mary and at last men knew what it was to be a man.

That was the tidings of great joy which saves life from being merely futile and warrants us in moving towards the future in a spirit of joy. No matter what our fears we are, after all, oriented to the future despite ourselves, biologically in our nature and humanly in our culture. It is into the future that men and women eat and drink and make love and rear children; dig gardens and build houses and paint pictures and write books. Despite ourselves and because of ourselves we are animals who are directed forward, who live future-wise. Yet that future can seem not so much a promise as a threat, looming up before us as no more than a succession of repeated pasts, different in detail but unaltered in quality. The future can seem condemned already before it comes to absence of meaning and futility, succession without significance and therefore most certainly one *damned* thing after another, alien, not ours, inhuman, unredeemed. To be future-oriented leaves open the possibility of futility, insignificance and ultimately despair. And it is into this condition of things that the gospel sends out its first word: 'Rejoice, Mary, filled with grace: the Lord is with you!'[9] The deepest meaning of the virgin birth of Jesus is that he is not simply the product of human evolution but is a new beginning. That is news which meets head-on our fears, suspicions, doubts and cares. It is a gospel or good news addressed to real men, men as they are, men threatened by despair. Christian joy, the joy which is a fruit of the Spirit, an indication of a man's steady maturing in the christian life, is far different from jollity. It is not gallant and high-hearted happiness. When our happiness is menaced by the threat of a

23

meaningless future and yet within that threat a man rejoices: that is what we call christian joy. To believe and hope and rejoice we are not asked to suppress or hide or refuse to look at our doubts and despair and angst. We are asked to take our unbelief, our inability to hope and our sense of the threat of the future into truly christian faith, hope and joy. We are invited to take our unbelief about what kind of a God God is, if indeed there is a God, into the heart of our faith and let it become part of what gives structure to our faith. We are invited to take our despair about the world and the church and our angst about ourselves and make it all part of the structure of our hope and joy.

Christian joy results from an option, from choosing to say that life has a meaning, even though the only name we can give that meaning is Jesus of Nazareth. All we have to go on is the word of God; that is, the fact that a handful of people have dared to speak in the name of God and to tell us that God promises that in the end it will not be just one damned thing after another,for history is a history of redemption. He who came in Jesus of Nazareth will come again in him: that is the promise we have elected to live by. Joy results from the expectation of an end which will give meaning to all that precedes it, as the final movement of a symphony gives meaning to the opening chord and all that follows. Ultimately, the coming again of Jesus is what our faith, hope and joy stand or fall by. Meditating on Jesus' first coming offers a language for speaking of his second coming to bring in his kingdom of peace and justice.

It was with a truly biblical instinct that the church in early times formed the calendar we have for acting through the liturgical year. At Easter nothing is allowed to get in the way of celebrating the death and resurrection of Jesus. But at Christmas every effort seems to be made to clutter up the time with other commemorations. Christmas day for just one day. Then the stoning of Stephen, followed by John the Divine, theologian and contemplative. Finally, the holy innocents, massacred because Jesus had come. The language of his first coming is a language of death and persecution as well as of births and shepherds, wise men and carolling angels. It is a language of swords to murder babies and swords to pierce the heart of Mary; a language of the stony heart of Herod and of stone for stoning Stephen. The loss of the child Jesus in the

24

Temple in St Luke's gospel gives us perhaps, the clue we need. The passage is a most skilfully composed overture to Luke's presentation of the origins of the christian faith in his Gospel and The Acts of the Apostles, including all of his major themes. The loss takes place at Jerusalem at Passover-tide, when and where the Lord was to be crucified. It 'must be',[10] as the passion and death of Jesus must be. People involved in this incident fail to understand what he is about, seek him and find him on the third day; as his own will do when he is killed and raised. At the finding there is the same sort of questioning – 'Why were you looking for me?'[11] 'Why are you looking for the living among the dead?'[12] In the infancy stories there is already present the passion, death and resurrection of Christ: Jesus the child grows in stature, and growing learns to die. The first coming is meant to prevent us from making too light of the second. We have to see the reality of the threat beneath which faith, hope and joy lie. The story of Stephen, and the Innocents and the three days' loss of Jesus teach us to interpret the very darkness of the world as a sign of Christ's coming. We are not to think that Jesus comes only in the manner of Dickensian christmas parties.

The good tidings of great joy of the one who comes were meant first of all for those who were really poor and afflicted, not for people like us for whom being poor and afflicted is most of the time a contrived spiritual state. The gospel was meant for people like Mary who in the Magnificat says that the Lord has looked on the affliction or humiliation or scorn of his slave-girl. The word used is the same as for the situation of the slaves in Egypt, when it is said that God looked upon their affliction, toil and oppression. The gospel was not for people who could cope, so it seems Christ did not come nor will he come for people like ourselves. Yet we are told that the gospel is meant for all men. It is the answer to the kink, bias and distorted gravitational pull that drags us where we would not go simply in virtue of being born into the world. It will only come to us as good news, however, if we are in some way amongst those to whom the kingdom is directed, the poor, the hungry, those who weep, those who are reviled on account of the Son of Man. We can find ourselves interpreted to ourselves in this language of stones, swords and broken hearts, and then hear the good news. Perhaps we can find ourselves bound at the coming of Jesus and then be able to rejoice with Mary

25

because his coming looses us. Perhaps we can come to see ourselves in the man who was born to die, and then find that his dying sets us free. Perhaps we can make more of saying Amen to the broken body and outpoored blood of Christ in the Eucharist than a ritual act, and find with Augustine that in saying Amen to that broken body we are saying Amen to what we ourselves are as individuals and communities and even as God's church. That will involve not only a death through water, baptismal living, but also a life in fire, accepting our purging and re-making by the Holy Spirit in the pentecostal gifts, the gifts of confirmation.

3

Confirmation

Jesus of Nazareth, the Christ of our faith, is the saving grace of God given a local habitation and a name. He is the Immediator of God and man, the one in whom there is no distance between what it is to be God and what it is to be man. He is the self-expression of God in the flesh, in the world, in history. As a man lives in the word he pronounces so in his Word, Jesus Christ, God is articulately present among us. Jesus is God's way of being the poet of the creation, revealing its capacity to symbolise and to undergo transfiguration. By words and ritual gestures we enact that meaning for ourselves and for one another.

One way in which we do this, as we have seen, is baptism, in which we submit to initiation into a new life. It is painful, as all initiations are. God's way of being human involved trusting himself entirely to us, and was realised historically at the moment when Jesus gave himself up to death at the hands of men. He entrusted himself to those who would betray him and kill him, and in and through and behind them to the Ground of all that is, the Father. It is this element in being human in God's way which we enact ritually when we allow ourselves to be baptised. Another element is that of living in and through the Holy Spirit, the power of God which can only be talked about in terms of wind and fire and water. This element is ritually enacted in our being confirmed. The reality of confirmation lies in the movement of life in the Holy Spirit.

Jesus from the first moment of his conception was altogether the work of the Holy Spirit. There was never anything about

Jesus which could be explained in terms drawn from Jesus himself, but all from the beginning had to be referred immediately to God. Jesus was conceived, we say, by the power of the Holy Spirit. The major moments of his life are presented to us as moments of being filled with the Holy Spirit: his baptism, his choosing of the apostles, his transfiguration, his offering himself in death, and above all his resurrection, when he becomes finally and fully the new humanity, God's way of being human. Jesus was raised by and in the Holy Spirit. Furthermore, as the apostolic preaching says, 'Being exalted at the right hand of God, and having received from the Father the promise of the Holy Spirit, he has poured out the Holy Spirit on us'.[13] He gives the inner dynamism of his risen life to us so that it may become the new life of our lives, the core of our personality, our new heart and soul, our new ego. The faith which is associated with baptism, that trusting of ourselves to another, is not all there is to be said about the christian life: we also have to think in terms of life in the Holy Spirit, of being interiorly transformed and becoming new people. The full process of christian initiation includes not only being baptised in water but some Spirit-rite, a laying-on of hands or an anointing, spoken of as connected with the gift of the Holy Spirit. God is not related to us simply as the one who arranges external circumstances in such a way that I am more or less inevitably drawn to love him and do his will; he is related to me as the one who is closer to me than breathing, nearer than hands and feet, and more interior to me than I am to myself. That is not altogether open to empirical observation. I cannot always look at what I do and see in its entirety the transforming work of God within me. What is in question is a new heart and soul. I have to be prepared to trust that God is transforming me in his own way in his own time, and to try as best I may to allow that to happen.

The Holy Spirit is the spirit who brings growth. Baptism is ill-equipped to express that. Baptism as simply trusting, just holding out our hand to God to save us of the depths, would be stunting and stultifying without the growth which is the work of the Holy Spirit. To become grown men and women in Christ we have to allow the Holy Spirit to activate us. What that will mean in detail cannot be legislated for or even anticipated. But we can get some idea by looking at some earlier manifestations. In the personal history of Jesus of

28

Nazareth, what was meant by Good Friday and Easter is the sort of thing that being baptised represents for us. What in the risen life of Jesus was meant by Pentecost is the sort of thing that being confirmed means for us. To be fully christian is to be a man of Whitsun as well as of Good Friday and Easter, to live pentecostally, in the spirit of Pentecost.

The work of the Spirit is to form within us that Christ who was sent out on a mission from his Father, the source of all that is and of his own personal existence. Being a christian of Pentecost means being equipped for ministry, becoming activated, getting beyond the latency period. 'You shall receive power when the Holy Spirit has come upon you; and you shall be my witnesses in Jerusalem and in all Judaea and in Samaria and unto the uttermost parts of the earth'.[14] the Holy Spirit has to do with witnessing to Jesus of Nazareth and what God has done in him. All his gifts are ordered to that end of witnessing to the good news in Jesus, which is good because it sets men free, healing and re-creating them and making them what they are to be.

When we think of the gifts of the Holy Spirit we usually think of gifts and graces that are unexpected, not to say a trifle odd. The typical such gift in the New Testament might be the gift of tongues, when a man remaining in full control of himself, able to speak or not to speak, chooses to speak without choosing the words he will say. Yet even that extraordinary gift when a free man is in a quite spectacular way given words to speak is a sign of all speaking about God. We open our mouths to speak the words God has given us, to speak them back to him or to other people, in the liturgy and in preaching or teaching. We are given what to say. It may be that the message of the gospel is given us in a charismatic way, so that the words seem to come to us. It is important that we cultivate a docility to being led in this way. But it may also be, and very often will be, a matter of craftsmanship and professional competence. We have no right to demand that words be given us when we are not prepared for the labour that is involved in acquiring and maintaining a professional competence, preparing lessons or sermons or whatever. The Spirit who gives men the gift of tongues is also the Spirit who is the source of our craftsmanship. For such preparation is no less the work of the Spirit than our being given the appropriate words unexpectedly, as Exodus makes clear: 'And Moses said to the people of

Israel, 'See, the Lord has called by name Bezalel the son of Uri, son of Hur, of the tribe of Judah; and he has filled him with the Spirit of God, with ability, with intelligence, with knowledge and with craftsmanship, to devise artistic designs, to work in gold and silver and bronze, in cutting stones for setting and in carving wood, for work in every skilled craft. An he has inspired him to teach, both him and Oholiab, the son of Ahisamach of the tribe of Dan. He has filled them with ability to do every sort of work done by a craftsman or a designer or by an embroiderer in blue and purple and scarlet stuff and fine, twined linen, or by a weaver – by any sort of workman or skilled designer. Bezalel and Oholiab and every able man in whom the Lord has put ability and intelligence to know how to do any work in the construction of the sanctuary shall work in accordance with all that the Lord has commanded'.[15] The variety of skills and techniques involved in, say, teaching are also gifts of the Holy Spirit of God and to be discerned as such, accepted with gratitude and cultivated. They too are ways of building up the kingdom of God, the true sanctuary which is the church of the living God, built up from living and chosen stones, the heavenly Jerusalem. All failure to discern, accept and cultivate the skills we have is failure in being a pentecostal, that is a confirmed, christian. Confirmation, our Pentecost, has committed us in advance to preaching in one way or another, directly or indirectly proclaiming the mighty works of God to others.

The Holy Spirit, as we can see from the experience of the apostles, gives us a new language in which to praise God either to others or to himself. A vital aspect of the gift of the Spirit of Pentecost is a new facility in praying. And here, in the matter of speaking of God to himself, it is the same picture as in speaking of God to others. Perhaps there will be spectacular and charismatic gifts; perhaps most of the time there will not be such gifts and prayer will appear as work. In either case what is requried is faithfulness to whatever the gift of the moment is, whether it is a gift of craftsmanship or of spon- taneity. There is a need to cultivate a sensitivity, therefore, to what gift God is giving: to learn to know when it is the time for free prayer, when for liturgical prayer, when to get out a book, when to shut up and be still in the presence of God, when to do not much more than sit in front of him and twiddle our thumbs. When we do not know how to pray, says Paul, 'the

30

Holy Spirit prays in us with sighs too deep for words, with unutterable groanings'.[16] In such times, the Holy Spirit takes over and does the praying for us if we will let him, if we will shut up and stop chattering at God. What matters is faithfulness in an attitude of readiness to let God be God, recognising that he has rights over and claims on us. The typically great men of prayer in the church, the Carthusian, the Cistercian and the rest, symbolise that claim by praying at the wrong times, in the middle of the night for example, when presumably they, like the rest of us, are in no fit state to talk to anybody at all, let alone to God. For us too, in our more relaxed régimes, the times when we must pray are often enough the wrong ones. To a busy housewife or working man, 7.30 a.m. may be quite as bad a time as two o'clock in the morning would be for a monk. And yet then too we are invited to let God be God. We can respond to that invitation in any number of ways, according to the rhythms of our constantly changing situation. At one moment fidelity will mean letting ourselves go when it seems we are being led into that, at another being craftsmen in our praying when it seems we are being led into that. Nowadays craftsmanship in prayer is at rather a discount. Yet it has its place and can be an antidote for being lazy about one's praying, for freewheeling and pretending it is the prayer of quiet. It is equally pentecostal, and so equally the authentic work of a confirmed, Spirit-filled believer, to pray with methods and to pray freely. If you are utterly parched and exhausted prayer may simply mean giving the Holy Spirit your body to groan in, as portrayed in the Nine Ways of Prayer of St Dominic.

The Holy Spirit, whose personal name is Gift, is the source of all gifts. 'Veni dator munerum',[17] we say to him: Come, giver of gifts. If we let the Holy Spirit become the life of our lives we have no idea where this might lead. The Spirit will give us gifts that have to be brought into play. The gift is a burden on us, it demands to be passed on. As with a chain letter, if you break the chain of passing on the Spirit turns sour and morbid; like the manna, the gift has grown worms by morning. But the gifts of this Holy Spirit who is so exacting with us are not entirely unpredictable. It is not as though you can say nothing at all about what would count as a gift of the Holy Spirit. We know that the Spirit is the spirit of Jesus, the real presence of Jesus, who is a name, a story, an event, a history and a biography. So by the test of Christlikeness there will be certain styles of behaviour which cannot on any count be regarded as appropriate to those who have the Holy Spirit. What that will mean positively is not quite so clear, although it must mean that the person who receives the Spirit becomes Christlike and a vicar of Christ to others. It is also clear that the gift above all gifts is charity. That is a more excellent way than all the charisms combined and the way without which those special gifts and graces are sterile or even devilish. Yet charity, christian love, is not much help in talking about what the gifts will mean, since it is the soul and sense of all the gifts rather than one amongst others. Paul tries from time to time to spell out something of what being another Christ by the Spirit might mean for us. He speaks of such gifts as the word of wisdom, the word of knowledge, faith, gifts of healing, miracle-working, prophecy, discernings of spirits, tongues, interpretation of tongues. Or he speaks of the variety of functions in the christian fellowship as gifts: 'first apostles, second prophets, third teachers, then workers of miracles, then healers, helpers, administrators, speakers in various kinds of tongue'.[18] All of these are for the building up of the body of Christ. As well as these institutional gifts there are the fruits of the Spirit: 'love, joy, peace, patience, kindness, goodness, faithfulness, gentleness, self-control'.[19] Paul speaks of the fruit of the Spirit, in the singular case. The gifts, it seems, are given to be integrated into a single personality. What goodness or faithfulness will mean for one of us is different from what it will mean for another. But in each instance it is there for wholeness, for the building up of the individual christian and of the community of believers. We shall see how the Holy Spirit is working in us when we see his fruit. It is interesting to note that this is a horticultural metaphor, in distinction from the industrial metaphor of the works of the flesh. The fruits are the result of a long and steady growth of ourselves in the Holy Spirit and of the Holy Spirit in us. They are the result of his unspectacular being with us and of his charismatic gifts, gifts given to each for the good of all.

To be a pentecostal christian is to use the gifts you are given for the good of all. What above all was wrong with the church in Corinth, as it appears in the pages of Paul's correspondence, was that people used the gifts which were from the Holy Spirit for their own personal enjoyment. They spoke in tongues in the full gathering of the church, for example, without caring about what good or harm this did anybody else. The Second Vatican Council has some wise words on the matter: 'Individual believers, according to the gift each has received, may administer it to one another and become good stewards of the manifold grace of God. From the reception of these charisms or gifts, including those which are less dramatic, there arise for each believer the right and the duty to use them in the church and in the world for the good of mankind and for the building up of the church. In so doing, believers need to enjoy the freedom of the Holy Spirit who breathes where he will. At the same time they must act in common with their brothers in Christ'.[20] This sensitivity to the requirements of one another is one of the key requirements in any spiritual living together, in any living together in the Holy Spirit of God. It is itself a gift of the Holy Spirit who is both the unity of the Father and the Son and the unifying force of the church. When we say at the end of the great prayer of thanksgiving in the Mass that through Christ and with Christ and in Christ all glory and honour is given to the Father in the unity of the Holy Spirit, we are touching on this double unifying work of the Spirit. He is the personal unity and love of Father and Son, but the phrase 'the unity of the Holy Spirit' can also refer to the church, where all glory and honour is given to the Father through the Son. The Holy Spirit is the soul of the body of Christ which is the church. He is literally the 'esprit de corps' of the christian fellowship. To be a pentecostal christian is to have a concern for the unity of the brethren both in the church universal and in that realisation of the church which is the community in which we live. The gifts to be sought are those which make for the building up of the body.

For the gifts can be sought: they may and should be prayed for. That is clear from Paul, and from liturgical sources where, for example, we find the tridentine Missal encouraging us to ask for such charisms as the gift of tears. Through the Holy Spirit himself we have the confidence to come before God boldly and to ask him for what we need. When we do that the altogether unexpected can happen. Then the good news is set loose in the world again, and the dry bones of our churches can be clothed again with flesh and skin and stand on their feet, an exceeding great host. Then the Spirit can appear in signs and wonders, as a new style of human life which is a colony of heaven, where people live together in peace, joy, love and kindness, learning to trust each other and to find God in each other. Then people are as God for one anotheer. Then Jesus of Nazareth is bodied forth again in this world and there is a new creation.

4

The Baptism of Jesus

All of us in some way or another have heard the call of Jesus of Nazareth to follow him; simply in virtue of letting ourselves be called christians we have expressed our general readiness to go along with that call, entering upon the way of discipleship. Following Christ is more primordial than imitating him. The New Testament is prepared to use the language of imitation now and again but the imitation, the copying, is set firmly in the context of discipleship, the following. 'Let this mind be in you which was in Christ Jesus' is its characteristic imperative, not 'Do the things that Jesus did'. There is nothing to be said for having been born in a stable, sentimentally appealing though the idea might be. There is nothing to be said in favour of the best kind of christians being carpenters, though no doubt if you happen to be a carpenter it might be quite a consoling thought that Jesus of Nazareth was one. There is nothing to be particularly recommended in having children baptised in water from the river Jordan, though no great harm is done if they are. Following after Jesus, seeing the possibility of a new way of living, is what is first and foremost in question rather than imitation. This means that some points in Jesus' life-story are likely to have more significance for us than others, for they will have more to tell us about what is involved in being a disciple. The key moments in his life have a significance out of all proportion to the others: by and large these are the moments which have become the object of liturgical celebration in the church, above all Easter and Christmas. It seems a pity that other special moments in Jesus' story have not been recommended to our constant meditation in the way in which the mysteries of his birth, death and resurrection have been. There are not usually five mysteries of the life of Jesus in the rosary, for instance, although people often extend that way of praying to keep before their eyes some such key moments. If you were given the job of deciding which five mattered most there should be little doubt that one of the key moments would be the baptism of Jesus.

Two of the gospels begin what they have to say about the life of Jesus there, omitting his childhood and youth. When Peter in the Acts of the Apostles suggests before Pentecost that the other ten should elect another apostle, the criterion he demanded was that the candidate, in addition to having been an eye-witness of the risen Jesus, should have been with him from the time of his baptism by John in the Jordan. The apostolic preaching in Acts often starts with that point. Even for Matthew and Luke, who have things to say about the birth and childhood of Jesus, the baptism represents a highly significant moment. Luke, by repeating words used of the boy Samuel of old, 'He continued to grow both in stature and in favour with the Lord and with men',[21] insists that Jesus is made in all things like to us. He has to learn things as we have to learn things. He has to learn knowledge and he has to acquire insight. Jesus is not a monster, with the mind of God and the body of a man, half God and half man; he is altogether one of us as he is altogether one with God: true God and true man, as the catholic dogma puts it. The orthodox in the first christian centuries fought to say that everything human was shared by Jesus. They tended to talk of everything human in noun language – will, intellect and the rest. We live in an age of verbs, so that their style tends not to be ours. But the basic concern remains: if there is something in our human experience which Jesus did not in principle share, that would not be redeemed. It would remain outside any meaningful pattern of human life. Luke's repeated text is stressing that what Jesus shared with us includes the whole process of maturing, of developing slowly, so slowly, in what we know and what we understand and how we relate to one another and to God. Jesus made even process, even the way to the goal, into a meaningful affair. God has become man not only in the sense that he possesses all the items that go to make up a catalogue of what a man should have, but also in the sense that he has a personal history, a real biography which can make sense of our individual histories and biographies. Being on the way, being uncertain, not knowing, living with ambiguity, striving to find out what we should do and be, does not mean that we are at a distance from God; this too is part of our humanity, which is now for ever with God and in God. All that experience of living with uncertainties and ambiguities has been taken up into God's way of being human whom we call Jesus, and so has been declared part of the properly human condition, something from which we must not seek to be liberated too soon and too quickly. In being baptised we see God identified with men in their human condition in its fulness. He has made himself process and entered into ambiguity. Now he openly puts himself under the Law, under the same condition of being bound which binds everyone. As one of the gospel accounts puts it, Jesus was baptised in the baptising of all the people. The epiphany or appearing of God our Saviour is not now going to be by way of earthquake, whirlwind and fire, or even by the still, small voice of silence: it is going to be, rather, as man amongst men.

In John's baptism it is all men whom Jesus takes to himself. When a Jew accepted that baptism he put himself in the place of a non-Jew, for baptism was one of the essential means whereby a non-Jew entered Jewry. When Jesus accepted John's baptism he puts himself in the position of a sinner, for baptism was essentially the means whereby repentance for sins was signified. In accepting John's baptism, Jesus put himself into a relationship of identity with anybody and everybody in their concrete situation of estrangement and distance from God. And when Jesus had worked out his faithfulness to that, his corpse on the cross was the epiphany of the goodness and humanity of God our Saviour. There if nowhere else you see all men made one, in death. The baptism of Jesus sets the mood for and bears the mark of the whole gospel, signing it with the sign of the cross. It is Jesus only, as he ascends out of the water or as he is praying, who hears the voice saying 'You are my beloved Son; with you I am well pleased'.[22] So too all through the gospel it will remain hidden that Jesus is in truth God's Son, made Christ with the Holy Spirit. What is known to Jesus alone at his baptism and through his ministry will be publicly recognized only at his crucifixion, when we will be lifted up by God and the signs at

37

his baptism made visible and audible for everyone. As Jesus saw the heavens torn apart at his baptism, so at his cruxifixion the veil of the temple is torn apart, the veil which hid God from man. As Jesus heard the heavenly voice proclaiming his Sonship so the centurion at the foot of the cross says to all who would listen, and to all who would later hear the gospel read, 'Truly, this man was the son of God'.[23] The crucifixion is signed on the whole public life of Jesus by his being baptized in Jordan river.

In that moment of his baptism, we see a privileged expression of our faith in the true structure of reality. In that moment when we see what it is to be Man, we see also what it is to be God, the threefold God. In the voice from heaven, the dove and the human body of the Word lies a revelation of the inner life of the godhead. We see that the meaning of Jesus is not exhausted in talking about Jesus as such, for what he is has in and behind it the Father and the Holy Spirit. We are dealing here with three inseparably interlinked stories. First there is a story about Jesus, about his birth and his growing up, about how he was made in all things like to us, about his baptism and the death and resurrection implicit in that. Second there is the story about the one we call the Father, a story of the coming to be of the world, the long evolution of mankind, the history of men with men and of God with men and more particularly the history of Israel among the nations. Thirdly, there is the story of our experience of the christian life, our own and that of the christian centuries before us. In the end, if any of these stories is told without the others it is told amiss. The Jesus story does not make sense except as part of a story about Israel; and neither story makes sense unless when you tell the story you talk about God. And so with that third story, the story of and about the Holy Spirit: this is a story about life in the church, about the power that possesses believers, re-creating and renewing them not just in pious sentiment but in all reality, as we find in the classic conversion stories like Paul's and Augustine's. This story too is mistold if it is not narrated in the context of the story of Jesus, which in turn only makes sense if you can speak of the Father as you tell it. To cut free the story of the Holy Spirit in Holy Church from the Jesus story as the apostles told it, thus making present experience independent of this last would be to make shipwreck of the faith. You need to be a pentecostal christian, for

38

the story of Jesus cannot be told without talking about Holy Spirit; but you are not a pentecostal christian if you cut off Pentecost from Good Friday and Easter. The Spirit is the Spirit of that Jesus who, in his baptism by John, took on the form of a servant. If it is really Christ that the Holy Spirit is forming in us then we too will have to bear the form of the Servant in the world like Jesus, who took to himself the whole human condition and claimed no special privileges.

The worst disservice we can do people is, in all probablility, to have Pentecost without Good Friday, to have a way of life which is not what we see in the event of Jesus being baptised in the Jordan. The way christians force people to despair is not by being ourselves unclear, muddled and at a rather a loss. It is by appearing to be none of those things, appearing already to know, to have arrived, to be certain, to have no need of the form of the Servant which belongs to the Jesus who is Christ.

5

The Sacrament of Forgiveness

Since Jesus of Nazareth, if we want to see what it would be like to be human we look at Jesus in his risen life, in that flesh of God which now reigns in glory, as the old breviary hymn puts it. But we have to see that there is there a new sort of human history, a new chapter in the story of man which makes it a new story, as the last chapter in a detective story changes the meaning of all the previous chapters. This new chapter reveals that the humanity we all share by being born is awry, with a gravitational pull away from where it ought to be. Man proves to be 'incurvatus in se', twisted in upon himself, the neurotic animal. That condition of human nature which we share just by being born as men amongst men has now to be left behind. We have to pass over into the new humanity, God's way of being human, which is now the only real humanity, Jesus of Nazareth. We have to return from the far country which is our old humanity to our Father's home, which is the risen body of Jesus. The far country where the prodigal son finds himself is the humanity which as creatures of flesh and blood we all share: to that country far from God the Word has come, becoming man in it, for there was no other place for him to become man except in that country far from God, except by becoming other to God. He took not the flesh of Adam before the Fall but my flesh, says St Bernard. According to Paul he was 'made sin for us',[24] 'sin' which comes from sunder, separation from God, alienation from oneself. Only out of the depths could he pray to God, since there was as yet no other place from which God could be called on. And then he came to himself,[25] and finding himself arose and went to his Father. Thereby Jesus became the new chapter which changes the whole of our history. He became the return of man to God. He lives now as that return made concrete, the sacrament of that return, the Immediator of God and man. We return to God insofar as we are united with him, involved with him, one body with him. That is symbolised and effected primarily in baptism, when we were made members of Christ, children of God and inheritors of the kingdom of heaven, being born a second time because by being born we had failed in our first birth.

From that point onwards, we should be living the risen life of Jesus, having his Holy Spirit as our spirit, the heart and soul of our new selves. But as yet the resurrection life is lived in promise, not fully achieved. It is still under threat, and it still remains possible for us not to allow the Holy Spirit of God to become our spirit. As yet it remains possible to stop trusting, and to lose that hold on God which we call faith. From the very beginning of the church this possibility has been recognised by christians. Even in New Testament times there were those who lost their hold on God in Christ, denying what they had received, that they were anything other than once-born. This happened most dramatically in times of persecution, when there was a kind of anti-sacrament to baptism which consisted in a man's making some gesture of worship to the powers of the state-religion. This created a tricky situation in the intervals between persecutions. There was a problem as to whether a man who had publicly denied Christ as the significance of his life could ever afterwards take part with those who had stood firm in that celebration of Christ as the significance of human life which we call the eucharist. The controversy was long and fierce, though eventually it was universally admitted that such a man might be readmitted to the fellowship of believers and that, in principle, any number of times. No sin was so great that it debarred a man from repentance and return. The three great sins which could have been regarded as being too great were apostasy, murder and public adultery: three ways of denying before men key aspects of the significance of Christ for the world. From those guilty of such sins some ceremony of return was demanded. A person who had denied Christ so publicly could not simply slip back into affirming him at the eucharist. The final development was the

41

acknowledgement that no sin was too small to be made the subject of a ceremonial return. Any sin is in some degree apostasy, a failing in our total commitment.

When we think of the sacraments we should always think of their celebration in its fulness. When we are thinking of the sacrament of second return, the sacrament of the forgiveness of post-baptismal failure, we should think not so much of the one-to-one encounter in the box, through a grille darkly, as of the enactment of God's love for sinners which can be found in the Roman Pontifical. On Maundy Thursday in that rite the bishop is to preside at a moving ceremony that culminates in a dance of the newly-restored penitents into the church from which they were debarred on Ash Wednesday. Or we can think of what used to happen in Spain on Good Friday, when as the story of the penitent thief was read out, the whole congregation began to shout out to the bishop to re-admit the public penitents to communion with the church. The sacrament as celebrated in such full ways is tremendously fruitful for meditation on what it means to sin after baptism and to be restored to the communion of the love of God which we call the church.

From such celebration we should be able to see that the church is the locus of forgiveness for even its own lapsed members. Forgiveness is part of the significance of Jesus of Nazareth for our world. Indeed in one perspective it could be said to be the significance of Jesus. One biblical framework refers to the forgiveness of sin as being the whole work of Christ. In the Fourth Gospel there is a scene in the Upper Room in Jerusalem on the evening of the first Easter Day which is really St John's version of Pentecost. The exalted Jesus breathes out the Holy Spirit on his disciples, saying: 'Receive Holy Spirit; whose sins you forgive, they are forgiven; and whose sins you retain, they are retained'.[26] The other gospels tell us how, at important points in his ministry, Jesus would say some such words as 'Your sins are forgiven';[27] they tell us how shocking this was to many people. They tell us how other people were glad and praised God who had given such power to men. To *men*, precisely. The purpose of the coming of Jesus, Jesus' taking man upon him to deliver man, Jesus' living amongst us with all grace and truth, Jesus' sharing our joys and crying when his friends died, Jesus' being betrayed with the kiss of friendship, the trial and condemnation, the death and three days in the darkness, and then the empty grave, was nothing other than the Holy Spirit. The first thing that the risen Jesus says of the Holy Spirit is that he comes for the forgiveness of sin. He himself is the remission of sin, as a collect in the Missal puts it. It was so that there might be this forgiveness, the personal presence of the Holy Spirit, that the long history of God's dealings with man took place.

The Holy Spirit is given to those who belong to Jesus so that they can, indeed must, forgive sins. The Holy Spirit is given to us as our very own spirit so that we can forgive sin for one another and be for one another the remission of guilt, the ending of burdens. We are called and required to be vicars of Christ for one another in the one Vicar of Christ, who is the Holy Spirit. What kind of cash-value can be given to such claims? They cannot mean that our personal past ceases to be what it was, nor that our mistaken, wrong-headed and downright wicked actions cease to have been such. But forgiveness means that we are no longer restricted by such past actions. We do not continue to be forced along by the ineluctable march of events. We are not entirely the captives of our own past choices. Somewhere, no matter how small a place it is, where the Holy Spirit has begun to be our spirit and has begun in some small measure to make us tick, there is a space where we are not determined by our past. That space is the locus where we can experience forgiveness, that experience of not being altogether creatures of our own making. If we do not communicate that experience to other people – if we do not absolve them – they remain bound. The forgiveness in question cannot be unmediated, though it is always unmerited. We are given the real presence of the Jesus story as our ego so that we can make a new beginning possible for other people. This involves not treating people as they expect to be treated, not indeed treating them justly at all, but being in their lives what they could not fairly expect. We must be towards them in a way consonant with the way other people have been pure gift for us, people we fall in love with and who quite astonishingly fall in love back. 'For-give' is the strengthened form of 'give', as 'par-donner' of 'donner' and 'ver-geben' of 'geben'. Christian forgiveness is a celebration of the sheer undeservedness of God's grace, which breaks the chain of purely causal connexions, of tit for tat and one good turn deserves another. 'If you do good to those who do good to you, of what profit is that to you? Do not the heathen do as much?'[28] The pure grace of the Holy Spirit, translating into our here and now the pure grace of the story of Jesus, is given to create a life-style which is not about doing good to those who are good, but of loving the unlovable, of forgiving the unrepentant, of not living with other people on the basis of their past, of being ourselves gift and grace for them.

Forgiveness of sins breaks the system, with wind and flame. It breaks the language barrier by a new possibility of communication through the diversity of personality types. It breaks the system by the unexpected and unlooked-for smile or word. It is not the caricature of forgiveness held out by Mr. Collins in Jane Austen's Pride and Prejudice who says, 'You ought certainly to forgive them as a christian, but never to admit them in your sight or allow their names to be mentioned in your hearing'.[29] There is a forgiveness which in no way breaks the system of a fallen world. Forgiving sin means having to do with people not as they are but as they might be, opening for them a future they have not yet seen. The art of christian living lies in making visible rather than in reflecting what is already visible, and in this it resembles the art of any good painter of portraits. If we can do this for people we shall be Jesus for each other and in the other we shall find Jesus for ourselves, him who is the altogether unmerited gift from the Source of all that is.

That is what allows the sacramental celebration of forgiveness in the church to make sense. If we do not give people some experience of what it is to be forgiven, and forgiven again and again, it is unlikely that they will make much of that privileged celebration of the forgiveness of God which is the sacrament of second repentance. One of the ways in which the life of Jesus comes to expression amongst us is as one baptised sinner forgiving another. This is ritually expressed in that gesture of solidarity which is the traditional centre of the rite: in the eastern tradition the two people – the one who will forgive and the one who will be forgiven – stand side by side before the representation of their common Lord in cross or ikon; and in the western tradition in the laying on of hands which is the old gesture of forgiveness. That was indicated in the old Roman rite by the raising of the priest's hands over the penitent. In the renewed liturgy of the sacrament the full gesture been restored. Laying on of hands, for whatever purpose

44

it is used, is a gesture of solidarity: solidarity in mission and commissioning in ordination, solidarity in sin and in the Lamb of God who takes away the sin of the world in the sacrament of second repentance. It is also one sinner who forgives another. That is the point of Jesus' remarks about not judging. We are not asked to make believe that the other person has not done something foolish or hurtful or otherwise evil to ourselves or to someone we love. We are asked not to let that be the governing characteristic of our relation with him. We are asked not to set him over against ourselves (as the righteous ones), but to set ourselves on his side, ranging ourselves with him and experiencing his wrong deed as something that diminishes us who are involved in it. This is typified in the gesture whereby Jesus identifies himself with the leper by touching him, by laying on of hands. We cannot be of any use to people in need if we refuse solidarity with them and insist on living with them at the level of the expectations we have of them.

A pentecostal christian must forgive: if he does not he is not himself forgiven. The most presumptuous prayer we ever make is the 'Our Father', which we could not have the courage to say unless the Holy Spirit said it in us. We find ourselves saying, 'Forgive us our trespasses as we forgive those who trespass against us'.[30] This is not a question of a bargain whereby I forgive someone and in return expect God to forgive me. There is, rather, a coincidence of the experience of forgiving and of being forgiven. When I finally forgive someone the wrong he has done me and my resentment of hours, days, months or years falls away, I in that very act have the experience of being myself forgiven. I am set free from the weight of crushing resentment, free to be in fellowship once more with him and with many another person besides. I cannot be freed from that burden as long as I refuse to free the other person. Forgiveness is an atmosphere we breathe.

But even so it can and should have its high, celebratory moments. Between the world and God lies a revolt, not a contradiction. So we can return and make that return into an occasion. This happens in an undramatic way at the beginning of each Mass, when we say in general terms to one another that we have failed in what we have thought and said and done and left undone, and then the forgiveness of God is called down upon us. It also happens in the penitential ser-

45

vices which the church nowadays celebrates at such times as Advent and Lent and the eves of major feasts. And most strikingly there is the sacrament of penance in the strict sense – what we call going to confession, the one-to-one encounter where one of the ones is a minister of the church. There is no doubt that this form of celebrating the mercy of God has been in crisis for some time now. We would do ill to critise anybody else's style of confession-going, for here there must be freedom for each to decide if, when and how often he will come to terms with himself as a sinner and with God as forgiveness in this particular way. But it would be odd if a person never did so. So it might not be amiss to say a word or two about the one-to-one celebration of the sacrament.

What we do in going to confession is to say something like, 'Look, God, this is the sort of person I am; I recognise that this is not the kind of person I ought to be and in my heart of hearts want to be. I know that there is the possibility of not continuing to be this kind of person'. But how do I know the kind of person I ought to be? There is no harm from time to time in looking at the Ten Commandments. If you are doing the kind of things that they rule out, you can scarcely claim to be acting very lovingly. Still, they are no more than a boundary line. More important is the failure to be the kind of person you are called to be. The jewish tradition behind our faith insists not that all men are created equal but that all men are created unique. The question that will be put to me is not 'Why were you not St Dominic?' or 'Why were you not Vincent McNabb?' but 'Why were you not Geoffrey Preston?' I get to know what it would mean to be myself from any number of hints and suggestions. I can look at the Beautitudes and see whether I belong with those to whom the Kingdom of God belongs, the poor in spirit, the meek, the peace-makers and the rest. I can look at Paul's description of the normal development of the christian character in the list of the fruits of the Holy Spirit, and ask myself whether, for example, I am joyful. I can look at the character-sketch of Jesus the universal man which is implicitly contained in Paul's Hymn to Love, and ask myself whether I am patient and kind, whether I seek not my own, whether I rejoice with all good men when truth prevails and the rest. I can reflect on my life with the help of those numerous ways in which people reflect on the human condition: read a good novel, or go and see a good film. But however we find out the truth about ourselves — and, just now and again, why not go and ask your best friend to tell you? — that is what we bring to confession, to another christian who is a failure like ourselves. In telling our story we are praising God, for we are confessing the mercy and love of God which is there even for such a person as me. We must tell the story the way it is, with compassion for ourselves and not masochistically, not pretending that we have been heart and soul in an unfortunate act into which it would be truer to say we have fallen. Yet in telling it we need not pretend either that the only things that we need to regret are those we have done with full deliberation. In either case we bring them to God and hear another sinner speak for God, telling us that we are forgiven, that we are not bound by what we have done, for there is a future for us beyond our right to expect, we who live in the good news that Jesus of Nazareth has been raised from the dead.

6

The Temptations of Jesus

It is in following Christ that we are pledged to working out what it means to be ourselves. What we are called to be can be seen throughout the life of Jesus made available to us in the gospels. That life, like any historical existence, was lived at a particular place, a particular time and with particular people: it is then and not now, there and not here, those people and not other people. But in being brought into language and made scripture it is removed from the particularity of there and then and those, and brought into the possibility of being here and now and these. All of his life that has entered into language is offered to us to become the life of our lives. 'Now Jesus did many other signs in the presence of his disciples which are not written in this book; but these are written so that you may believe that Jesus is the Messiah, the Son of God, and that believing you may have life in his name'.[31] There is the extraordinary story of Jesus' being driven into the desert by the Holy Spirit. He is driven into the wilderness to learn to come to terms with what he had, in principle, committed himself to in his baptism in the Jordan. There he was to wrestle with what people expected of the one who was going to be the form of the Servant for them, their Messiah. He had to wrestle with the fantasy-life of his people, those who – with the best will in the world – expected something which he was not sure they had a right to expect. It would be a matter for surprise if we never experienced such a struggle to find out whether accepting a rôle, and meeting the expectations of others, is to be faithful to the inspiration of the Holy Spirit in our own lives, or is to betray it. The temptation involved is not always between the bad and the good but, much more subtly, between good and better, or better and best. We too will at some point or other find ourselves forced into this wrestling with our individual and group fantasies and driven out into the wilderness where there appear to be no landmarks or directions, into that dry, thirsty land without water when man feels an alien. How may we learn from the gospels what it is to follow Christ in such situations?

The account of the temptations of Jesus is a 'legendum', something requiring to be read, words which in being read give us access to the mystery of Christ's struggle with the pressures of his world. The versions in the New Testament go out of their way to suggest that they are highly stylised renderings of what was a constant throughout the ministry of Jesus. In Luke's gospel, the Devil departs from Jesus 'until an opportune time'.[32] But this opportune time seems to be each and every crucial moment in Jesus' ministry, for at the Last Supper he looks back over the entire period as a long series of temptations. 'You are those', he says to his disciples, 'who have continued with me in my temptations'.[33] At each crucial moment he had to affirm freely what he had said ceremonially about himself in being baptised by John. The opportune time par excellence for the Devil, the truly and literally crucial time, was the moment of the crucifixion. Then Satan entered into Judas who is called Iscariot. While Jesus is dying on the cross the desert temptations flood back again. 'If you are the Son of God, command that these stones be made bread, cast yourself down from the Temple, worship me'. And now, once again, 'If you are the Son of God, God's chosen one, the king of the Jews, the Christ, save yourself and us'. Here in full force was the threat to his integrity that stemmed from the fantasies of others.

He was tempted in all things as we are tempted, the Letter to the Hebrews tells us. He was tempted in the desert, far away from the familiar and with nothing to rely on except what we also have. Jesus and the Devil dispute like a couple of rabbis, shooting texts at each other, but the Devil is the bright boy, the one with the original ideas. In all probability he will win, by inducing in Jesus a failure of nerve or an overweening confidence in his own capacities. Jesus would accept the challenge and test his assurance that he was the Christ by subject-

49

ing it to empirical observation; or, alternatively, he could be daunted by the possibility that the empirical observations might turn out to be negative, abandon faith in his mission and go back home to start planing wood again. Israel had failed like that in the desert for forty years, either by bluster or by loss of nerve. The story of the temptations of Jesus is a tissue of quotations from the literary deposit of that old encounter between the Devil and God's chosen one, Israel. So God's chosen one, Jesus, was on unfavourable ground. The field of battle was not picked by him but chosen for him. He was driven by the Spirit to the only possible tempting-ground, the desert where his people had lost before and in losing had lost themselves. He has even less encouragement than they, for they had manna and water from the rocks and a rough-tough Moses to lead them on. Jesus had nothing: his situation was ours, with the manna only a day-dream, the rocks rock-hard and no more charismatic leaders around.

The three temptations in Matthew and Luke typify the forms in which the temptation to loss of nerve or undue self-confidence come. What the three have in common is the way that people want a Christ, a Saviour, a God, after their own heart, in their image and likeness, in keeping with the fantasies of the time as to what a Christ, a Saviour, a God should be. Let us look at them a little more closely.

Firstly, 'If you are the Son of God, command these stones to be made bread'.[34] That is, people expect the golden age to be one of prosperity and plenty. But is not that part of the jewish and the christian hope, the messianic banquet for all nations? There are two ways of perverting that hope by temptations. One is to refuse to see that the business of bread has anything to do with us at all: we could opt for a kind of living which was untouched by the simple material needs of other people. The other, which is the stronger nowadays for us as it was for Jesus, is to satisfy those needs and spend all our time so doing. There could be no messianic age without prosperity, but prosperity does not make a messianic age. Feeding bodies and minds is good: but it is a temptation to think you are thus saving people. To give people bread and circuses and to be content with that is to treat them as animals rather than men; to feed them with information according to the best modern methods so that they can be a credit to themselves and to their families, and to be content with that, is to treat them like

50

computers rather than men. Being messiah includes resisting that fantasy. Man shall not live by bread alone, whether from the bakery or from the language laboratory: he will live by every word that proceeds from God's mouth. Bread for the body and the mind must be accompanied by bread for the spirit, bread that will enable people to attain the measure of the stature of the fulness of Christ, who is God's way of being man.

But there are other ways in which Jesus could accept that people were wholly right in their fantasies and give them what they want. When the Messiah comes will not the blind see, the lame walk and the tongue of the dumb shout for joy? The old texts say that when Messiah comes the wilderness and the solitary place will be glad, the desert will rejoice and blossom as the rose. If there is going to be a messianic age, will not wonders be done? Why, then, should not Jesus do a spot of wonder-working? If he cannot throw himself off the Temple, doesn't that imply that he doubts the truth of the voice he thought he heard saying, 'You are my beloved Son, you are my chosen One?'[35] Does it not suggest that he was less than wholly in it when he committed himself into the hands of the Father at that baptism in Jordan? Yet Jesus was in a way prepared to put God to the test. One of the things that struck people was that he healed: some at least of the blind saw, some of the deaf heard, some of the lame leapt for joy because of him. Why should it be a temptation to throw himself off the roof of the Temple into the hands of his Father, trusting to be held up by him, when it was no temptation, seemingly, to walk on the waves of the sea towards his disciples in a storm-tossed boat? The reason must be that what he was being tempted to do in the desert was something that would merely impress people without changing them. It was a temptation to give a fireworks display that would leave people unchanged in themselves, perhaps coercing them into admiration or awe-struck fear but in the end only mystifying and alienating them. Throughout his life Jesus has to resist this temptation to lead those who were impressed but not altered. It is the same temptation which we know, especially the professional christians amongst us, to impress people with our learning or our plant or whatever, without really changing them: we thus make them less capable of doing things for themselves and less free to discover what it is they need to do, for they are being

51

kept in a prolonged childhood or adolescence. It is when there is a question of people's need that the time comes to act with confidence, to hold God to his word in the trust that he will see his beloved children through a situation where the work is for the real good of others. What is required in us is the sense to discern people's real needs and how to meet them, to be where we are needed in our work and not where we are not.

The third typical temptation is the temptation to have power by the Devil's means. 'All this I will give you if you will fall down and worship me'. In the New Testament the Devil is called 'the god of this present age'. The Devil can offer power and dominion if we will accept the structures of our present society, getting people in positions of influence to pull the strings that will obtain what we want. The most obvious form of temptation which we might scorn as individuals, yet as groups and communities be not uninclined to use, is getting on the right side of the Scribes and Pharisees.

But to these typical forms of temptation Jesus responds appropriately and goes on responding thus all through his life. He accepts that they have the force of alluding to things that are right and good, yet sees that in the form in which they present themselves they are devilish. The odds were against his succeeding, as they are against our succeeding. Nevertheless, despite the fact that people had failed so often in the past and despite the Devil's greater versatility in presenting his case, it is Jesus who wins. He wins through sheer loyalty: he puts himself under the authority of scripture even when the Devil quotes scripture at him; he submits himself to the tradition of his people, being truer to that tradition that it was to itself. Jesus preserves his integrity by an entry in depth into what had made him what he was, as we must recover ours similarly. The loyalty of Jesus to the springs of his own being in history and amongst the people of God was more than verbal agreement, at times ran counter to verbal agreement. The Devil cited scripture. But in such loyalty Jesus found the source of his own being and so became what he was meant to be, God's way of being man.

7

The Sacrament of Healing

Jesus of Nazareth is the sacrament of man's salvation, the meeting of man and God, the very embrace of the Father and the returning prodigal. In being christian we are experimenting deeply in that way of being human which is the only real humanity, the humanity which God lives and whom we call Jesus. But to say that Jesus is the salvation of the human race sounds like using a highly specialist and churchy word. Salvation, far from being a term for authentic humanity, is not bandied round much outside church-buildings and the coteries of the pious. This is a pity, for originally it is not a pious word. To talk about salvation in the ancient christian languages of Greek and Latin – about sótéria, salus – is to talk about healing. Jesus is our Saviour because he is our Healer, the Good Samaritan, the Physician of the human race. Just as his work can be talked about as the forgiveness of sin so it can be talked about as healing. Jesus is our Healer or, more strongly, he is the Health of the human race, the healing and health. This you can do sacramentally in the sacrament of healing, which is one of the privileged expressions of the christian life to which we belong by our baptism.

Jesus is humanity as saved, restored and returned from that far country in which man lives estranged from God. One of the features of that country is that it is a disease-ridden land. In the Kingdom of God, so runs the promise, there will be no sickness or disease. Christians are supposed to live as a colony of the Kingdom, as people whose homeland is elsewhere, as displaced persons, as exiles, but with the way of life that belongs to their native country, God's terrain. Like so many colonials, however, they have a tendency to go native and adopt at least some of the features of life in the country they are in. They go native by sinning, and also by falling sick. In falling sick we christians show that the salvation which Jesus is has not yet achieved full control of our lives. Not that there is any question of sickness (my sickness) being a punishment for sin (my sin): normally there is no question of my sickness being my fault in any more significant sense than that I would not have caught cold if I had been prudent enough to take a mackintosh with me. But sickness amongst men is a sign that we are still in a far country and need to return to God. When God's Reign comes in all its power and death and hell are thrown into the lake of fire, there will be no more sickness. The nations will be healed by the leaves of the tree of life which is Christ's cross. Sickness is a sign of the continuing dominion of darkness, a kind of anti-sacrament, an effective sign of the present evil age. It is indecent that a christian should be ill, downright 'in-decens', unfitting and unbecoming. Nowhere in the scriptures do we find a person being encouraged to reconcile himself to this illness, to put a good face on it and accept it as God's will. Instead, people are encouraged to seek healing, to seek already to be able to live as citizens of that coming Kingdom when the eyes of the blind shall be opened and the ears of the deaf unstopped, when the lame man shall leap as the heart and the tongue of the dumb sing for joy, when people shall no longer be oppressed by their bodily infirmity. In the days of his flesh Jesus both forgave sin and healed sickness. Those two facets of his work continue sacramentally in his body the church: there is a sacrament of forgiveness and a sacrament of the healing of sickness. As in being baptised we are setting ourselves in line for a life-long dying, as in being confirmed we are setting ourselves to be pentecostals, so in being members of a church that claims to forgive and to heal, we are committed to the work of forgiveness and healing.

Probably healing is more of a stumbling-block than forgiveness because it is so obviously a change in the real world and not simply an inner change which might be no more than a mask of words. The intrusion of God's Kingdom upon the present world cannot leave this world unchanged. In his miracles Jesus takes it by storm. The church is entrusted with continuing this work of changing the empirical world-order

54

and claiming more and more of it for God. Paul speaks of healing as one of the gifts of the Holy Spirit. Stories of healings crop up throughout the Acts of the Apostles. James lets us see something of a healing rite in the church, when the representative figures of the local church are called in by the sick man to anoint him with oil and to pray over him. The prayer of faith will heal him, says James. The elders take a gesture which was a perfectly ordinary one in the care of the sick at that time – like rubbing him with Sloane's linament, let us say. This becomes in their hands an effectual sign, a sacrament, of the care of the Lord Jesus for the sick man. The care in question is aimed at his healing, in that way making him fit for the Kingdom of God. The Catechism of the Council of Trent notices that quite often people in its own day were not recovering when the sacrament was celebrated; it ascribes this to the weak faith of a great part of those anointed with holy oil or of the ministers, not to any defect in the sacrament. The sacrament aims at healing. We belong to a church which expects people to be healed physically by Christ and which in Christ's name cares for them so that they may be healed. We belong to a church which expects her Lord's activity to make a real difference in the real world, changing men's bodies as well as their hearts and souls.

This sacrament should alert us to the fact that redemption is to do with man in his bodiliness, in all that makes his man: social man, political man, economic man, sexual man. We are redeemed not out of but into our bodiliness. We are redeemed by being immersed more deeply in our common humanity which is rooted and grounded in a shared flesh and blood. Our bodies do not cut us off from other people but put us in communication with them. Being bodily is what makes fellowship possible, and so what makes humanity possible. Followers of Christ cannot refuse to be concerned with all that makes for human healing and renewal, that is, with such matters as the political struggle for peace and justice in the world. Not that the changes we may be instrumental in making will themselves bring in the Kingdom of God, by means of the world's getting better every day in every way. Christians must offer a critique of every kind of human society before the Lord comes. Similarly, though there is a sacrament of healing, all men will die until the Lord comes, even though at its best that dying like Mary's is a falling asleep, ripe fruit dropping off the tree.

The limitations built into the very structure of the sacrament should persuade us against over-ambitious expectations from the present world-order. But equally they compel us into caring for all that is sick and oppressed and endeavouring to heal it.

While it is true that we have to beware of living with people on the basis of our expectations of them rather than of what they are, the sacrament of healing urges us not to be without expectations for ourselves and for others. We are invited to seek again and again to be healed from that sickness which is our falling short of our full humanity, to be healed from that condition which is the whole body of mankind being less than the redeemed humanity it is meant to be and in principle already is, in the risen body of Jesus Christ. In our dealings with each other, therefore, we should entertain expectations of the other person. But we entertain them aright only when we are committed to creating the situation in which those possibilities in other men can be realised. It is no use going around the monastery, for example, thinking that Brother So-and-So should drop some infuriating trait of behaviour if the only way he can be anything at all is by his idiosyncracies and deviance, since we lean on him so much. Having expectations is only christian if it goes with having compassion. We cannot demand that the sick man get up and walk if we do not speak to him the words that release him from his lameness. We cannot make that demand if we lack the kindness and concern that invites him back into the community of the whole. 'Cure this your servant', the church prays. 'Heal his wounds; rid him of all anguish of mind and body; in your mercy give him back full health within and without, that by your goodness he may be well again and take up his former life. Give him back to your holy church that all may be well with him'.[36] For it to be possible for that prayer to be answered, it must be genuinely possible for the sick man to come back into the community. Taking up his former life could mean that he would simply become sick all over again, if the community in which his former life was lived is not welcoming, compassionate and a community of healing. Healing depends on the christian community. The sacrament is evidently the work of the community, if only in virtue of engaging those who are the community's representatives. 'Is any among you sick? Let him send for the elders of the church',[37] writes

James. A whole gaggle of them, presumably, like the seven priests in the Greek form of anointing the sick, or the large numbers who wander round anointing at Lourdes during the great celebrations of the sacrament there. It is as communities, as groups and parishes and monasteries, that we need to be concerned for our sick with compassion and understanding and real help, even with a readiness to reform in ways that could make a weaker member's return possible. A therapeutic community is one which exploits to the full the healing potential of each of its members.

In this respect it scarcely matters what form sickness takes. The gospel offers a diagnosis of the human condition in terms of a universal and pervasive sickness unto death, one man alienated from another and each man a stranger to himself. It sees each one of us as schizophrenic, split-minded. 'The good that I would, that I do not; the evil that I would not, that I do', as Paul puts it. 'I do not do what I want, but I do the very thing I hate. So, then, it is no longer I that do it, but sin which dwells in me. I delight in the law of God in my inmost self, but I see in my members another law, at war with the law of my own mind and making me captive to the law of sin which dwells in my members'.[38] Probably no one has ever described this phenomenon better than Paul himself. He defines for us the distance between a man's true self, what he would want to be, what is called here 'the law of his mind', and the man's embodiment. This distance or rivalry, as Paul calls it, is one of the ways in which we experience the fundamental sickness that afflicts us in being human: split personality, sick personality, man at war with himself. Healing must involve integration, the abolition of the distance betwen a man's best self, the law of his mind, and the embodiment of his self, the contrary law in his members. Holiness entails wholeness, which in turn implies healing. This is a healing prior to the individual sin. It is a restoration of the image of God in man in accordance with the Genesis myth of man as he was meant to be, at peace with himself, with the animals and with God. Healing has to do with the restoration of Adam, the taking up of the first Adam into the second Adam, Christ, who is God's way of being Adam, that is, Man. Then man will no longer be a stranger to himself but will be self-possessed, for he will be redeemed into being altogether at home in his body into a perfect coincidence of the spirit that is in man with the embodiment of that spirit in flesh and blood, which is man's way of being in the world and with other men.

Whatever we do, we must not opt for less than that healing, less than re-integration of ourselves, less than becoming fully at home in our bodies. To despise anything about ourselves would be to despise what God has made and made good, indeed very good, however much we may fail to use it aright. The experience of the inner distance between our selves and our embodiment tempts people to seek redemption outside the body, which is accordingly either ill-treated or pampered. But the meaning of asceticism lies in integrating the body and so coming to be truly at home in it. That requires not a technique but a transformation, the transformation of God's grace. In traditional theology grace has been referred to as 'gratia sanans et elevans', grace that heals and raises up; for the only way to be healed, ultimately is to be raised up. Such healing brings with it forgiveness and a going over, above and beyond what would otherwise have been. What has been lost can be found again, just as when children we knocked a precious vase off the mantelpiece and dreamed that by a miracle the broken pieces could be the vase again. 'I will restore to you the years which the swarming locust has eaten, the hopper, the destroyer and the cutter, my great army which I sent among you'.[39] Healing means being raised up, not just continuing to live. There can be no ultimate loss so long as the possibility of healing remains. Thus in the christian perspective it makes perfect sense to say, for example, that a person is not yet virgin rather than that he has lost his virginity. And no matter how continent a man may have been, that is not the same as having a pure heart, the undivided heart which coincides to perfection with the embodiment of its will. 'Blessed are the pure in heart', says the Lord, 'for they shall see God'.[40] The psalmist prays God to create a pure heart for him. The kind of heart that God requires of us he gives us as his free gift, a gift which is no less a work than the creation of the world itself. The fiftieth psalm balances so delicately on that word create, used in the Bible only for the action of God. We pray to God that he himself will act to abolish in us the inner space between what we would be and what we are. This he will surely do, if we let him. We can help that work in one another by love and friendship, yet the work is not ours but his. The work is his, but in him and under him we who have committed ourselves to a church that cares sacramentally for the sick must help create the situation in which our brethren can come to have purity of heart, and so be raised up to newness of life.

Nevertheless, as we know, people are not always healed. The outcome of sickness may not even be a falling asleep in the 'sleep of death that is marked with the sign of faith'[41] but may be a continuation of the sickness for years and years, with much pain and suffering. Paul himself had some kind of sickness (whether physical, mental or moral we have no way of knowing), which he prayed to have removed from him in a request repeatedly refused by God with the answer, 'My grace is sufficient for you'.[42] The answer is no answer to the implicit 'Why?' of Paul's prayer, but it should make us attend to an aspect as yet not touched on. If a man does not recover from sickness of mind or body or behaviour the care of Christ which the sacrament of healing enacts still can and should change the meaning of sickness for him. That is not all there is to be expected, but it is a part of the picture. If a man is not healed, that is not necessarily a sign of his lack of faith, for it may be part of that mystery in God's ways with men which cannot be fathomed. The failure of healing by no means argues God's absence or indifference. This is also important when we think of moral failings. No doubt very many of us have some particular moral failing which we recognise and would want to be without, but which is obviously something not that we do but that we undergo. It has every appearance of being outside our control, although we know that no one is compelling us to do whatever we do. We can sincerely repent of a bad habit, saying honestly that we want to be rid of it. In that situation we can fairly expect that we will be broken of the habit, and that the grace of God will heal and raise us. Yet it may be that the bad habit continues, with genuine sorrow and genuine love of God. What then? Surely we must go on wanting and praying calmly and not phrenetically to be rid of such thorns in the flesh (if we go berserk about them they will never go away: the healing after all is God's work). But ought we not also to try to discover what we can about the meaning of God's refusal to take away the thorn? We may not be able to find what the continuance of the habit is about, but then again we may. Paul seems to have got a dusty answer from God, although he hazards that the failing was to stop him getting too elated about his visions and special gifts, which perhaps suggests a moral fault. In our case it may be that the thorn is there so that we can learn greater compassion for others who wobble in different ways from ours, greater understanding, tolerance and love; despite everything the love of God can be experienced in and through the habit. Unhealed still, we may discover that we are not unloved.

The ways in which God's healing can come to us are without number. He can heal us even when we are asleep if need be. That extraordinary woman Thérèse of Lisieux has a long piece about what a good thing it is to sleep during meditation. In the Book of Genesis the Lord God puts Abraham into a deep sleep in order to make covenant with him. There is the setting for that most humane teaching of the church on purgatory, 'ecclesia dormiens', the sleeping church, as Nicholas of Cusa calls it. The church recognises that people may die with their wills and hearts and minds set for God and yet still mixed up and twisted in all sorts of ways. In the sleep of death God has time to heal them and renew them in the image of him who is the Health of the human race, Jesus Christ, God's way to be man. As we are committed to caring in love and compassion for those who are ill, so we are committed to continuing that care, love and compassion for them even when they have died. We are bound over to pray for them, to surround them with our love and concern so that the healing which has been effected by God in the core of their personalities may work right through them and become a reality in the whole of their being.

8

Highlights of the Lord's Ministry: through temptation to Transfiguration and Entry into Jerusalem

The New Testament has another way of presenting the temptation of Jesus, in addition to the theme of testing as Israel was tested for overweening self-confidence or for despair. Jesus may be seen as driven out into the wilderness by the Spirit not to be Israel but to be Adam, true man. 'O loving wisdom of our God / when all was sin and shame / a second Adam to the fight / and to the rescue came. . . . O wisest love, that flesh and blood / which did in Adam fail / should fight afresh against the foe / should fight and should prevail'.[43] Jesus was tempted as Adam. He was with the wild beasts as Adam was with them. The angels ministered to him, as in rabbinic speculation they ministered to Adam. The Jesus of St Mark's Gospel undergoes Adam's temptation to eat of the tree of the knowledge of good and evil. That temptation put to Eve by the serpent in the world first theological argument ('Did God say. . . .?') is perhaps the most fundamental of all. The creature promises that if the human couple eat of the tree they will be like God, knowing good and evil. They proceed to eat, and thereby find themselves cast out from paradise, from the situation in which they were created to be, from being at home with the beasts and the world of nature, at home with one another, at home with their work. These myths of Genesis are primarily concerned to describe rather than to explain. They say more about the way man is in the world than why he is that way. This particular one is saying that Adam, Man, just by being man is in a situation of alienation as the result of eating of the tree of the knowledge of good and evil. We know right from wrong: we live in a world in which we are constantly presented with choices, decisions about good and evil, about what to do and what not to do. We live in a moral universe, a world that comes to us in the shape of shoulds and oughts and musts. And that, so the Genesis myth says, is a fallen situation. Man in that situation is outside Paradise, outside the place where he is at home. Man was not created to live in a world of commandments, of 'This you shall do' and 'This you shall not do'. This is not what being human was meant to be, but it is the way being human is in fact. To have a super-ego, that interior taskmaster, that pharisee in the heart, is to be a fallen man. Man was not made for this, but for the life exemplified in the Kingdom of God where there is no question of should and ought and must. The blessed saints have passed beyond morality, transcending this ethical universe.

This is the temptation Christ has to face. Do I live on the basis of should and ought and must? In some ways ethical life is an easy style of living, since you know where you are, what is demanded of you, when you have done your duty and the rest. It is right that there should be standards of behaviour. We must not try to escape morality. Yet we must also see that it is not the truly human way. Christ Jesus passed through that ethical world, that world of learning to do the Father's will, into a world where he was no longer in the position of have and ought and should, when he was raised in the Spirit. St Thomas Aquinas gives us the clue to this passage when he says that it belongs to Christ and to those who are Christ's to do God's will with ease and joy and spontaneity. We are invited to learn to do the things that God has prepared for us to do not because we ought to do them, but because it comes naturally to do them in the fresh nature God has given us. St Benedict in his Rule holds out this same prospect to his monks. The monk 'will presently arrive at that love of God which (being perfect) casts out fear. Whereby he shall begin to keep, without labour and as it were naturally and by custom, all those precepts which he had hitherto observed through fear; no longer through dread of hell but for the love of Christ and of a good habit and a delight in virtue, which God will manifest by the Holy Spirit in his labourer'.[44] The philosopher Collingwood once said that the vanity of human wishes does not lie in men's desiring what is not to be had or what is unattainable by themselves, but in their being mistaken as to what they want. Those who follow Christ are invited to move continually through doing what they ought to do until they arrive at doing what it comes easily, naturally and spontaneously to do. The trouble about this doctrine is that we tend to think that being spontaneously ourselves is a simple matter, whereas it is quite remarkably difficult. It would be simple if what we are were a given, which our faulty upbringing, the mistakes of our parents, teachers and superiors have overlaid and distorted. (They can never do anything right, can they?) But what we are is not a given: it is a project, something to be achieved or, better, received. It is quite remarkably difficult to know what it would be like to inhabit a world that does not present itself to us morally, in which we cannot help but do the will of God. Spontaneity does not mean doing the things that our institutions forbid, or not doing the things they require. That would be to betray that we were still bound, prisoners of our own likes and dislikes. To do things that are required to be done is not the same as doing them because they require to be done. To carry out rules (or the Rule) because it is an ought, a should and a must is to opt for a less than human way of being man. It is to ratify the eating of the fruit of the tree of the knowledge of good and evil. This Jesus had to learn, in discovering how to do the will of his Father in such a way that it finally became his own will.

Christ had to learn this in all the details of his ministry. He faced continually the temptations to live according to the fantasies of his people or according to an externally imposed law. He had to learn how to internalise the commandments, perceiving that what matters is not the law of God (as other than God) but the will of God (which is God himself). We glimpse the struggle with the fantasies of his people most notably in one particular incident. Jesus had been praying and, as always happens when a person prays, he had been led into himself, led to find himself before God. When he had finished his prayer he said to his disciples, 'Who do people say that I am?'[45] They tell him that people are saying all kinds of nice things about him, that he must surely be one of the great prophets come back from the dead and all the rest of it. Jesus goes on to ask them what they themselves have to say about him. Peter takes the word for them all and acclaims Jesus as

the Messiah, the saviour the jewish nation had been awaiting.
Jesus responds by saying pleasant things about Peter's pers-
picuity, but then begins to explain what was involved in what
had just been said. He warns them not to go round using this
Messiah language, because he is sure that they have it all
wrong anyway. In case there was any doubt he spells it out for
Peter: it means in practice suffering, rejection and death. Peter
tries to stop him saying such dreadful things and gets called
Satan for his pains. What Peter really wanted was one expression of the fantasies of the whole people about the Messiah
who was to come. He wanted what Jesus was struggling
against all through his ministry: a Messiah who would be
Messiah economically, spectacularly and devilishly.

Eight days later – the next incident in the gospel story is
specifically related to this – Jesus took Peter, James and John
to a high mountain apart from the rest. There he was
transfigured before them. The disciples catch sight of the
figures of Moses and Elijah. Peter in his daze wants to make
three booths or tents for them, to do the proper liturgical thing
which he has been taught in the synagogue. It must be that
the Glory which had come in the Tent of Meeting in the desert
has returned to Israel. The promised age must have come. He
wants to do the liturgically approved thing. The answer is a
voice and a word, 'This is my beloved Son: listen to him'.[46]
The glory of Yahweh is enshrined now in Jesus, in God's way
of being man. This glory is presented for a moment in the
images of the cult, in which they would expect to see glory, the
dazzling light, the bright garments, ways that recall the coming of God's glory in ages long ago. But the emphasis shifts
from looking to hearing: 'Listen to him'. God's glory is
enshrined in the Jesus who is telling them that he is going to
suffer in Jerusalem as one yielded up to the pagans, mocked,
shamefully treated, spat upon, scourged and finally killed.
God's glory will be found in the face of a man made fun of, a
human face spat upon. It will be seen on a man's back when
the whip tears it open, on a man's body as it hangs dying, on a
corpse. God's glory, his self-revelation in worship, will be
known definitely in a suffering man. This corresponds to a
most fundamental jewish and christian pattern. God says to
Abraham that he will go down with him into Egypt; but his
presence there, according to Isaiah, consists in the fact that in
all the people's afflictions he was afflicted. Ezekiel sees the

Glory, the wheels within wheels, the fire that was full of eyes, but he sees it precisely among the exiles by the river Chebar sitting down by the waters of Babylon to weep for the loss of Zion. The glory of God may manifest itself in the cultic, but it cannot be confined there. It is where it wishes to be. We adore it properly in the sacred setting only if we can perceive it in the profane. St John Chrysostom, the Golden-mouthed, tells his people in Constantinople that it is no use overdressing Christ in the symbolic form of the altar when he is going round the streets in personal form so badly clothed. There is no use treating a chalice with reverence because it holds the sacramental blood of Christ if we do not reverence every person, inside and outside our communities and congregations and age-groups. These other people do not simply hold the sacramental form of Christ's life: they are his living limbs. The cultic is always ambiguous in Christianity, never self-justifying. If we make Eucharist when we are not in peace and charity with our neighbours then the real presence of the Lord which he has covenanted with us itself condemns us. 'I hate, I despise your solemn feasts', can be the word of God to us as it was to those to whom he spoke in his prophet Amos. 'Is this the fast that I choose?' we have read at us from Isaiah at the beginning of Lent. 'Is this the fast that I choose, a day in which a man humbles himself, when he bows down his head like a bulrush and spreads sackcloth and ashes under him? Will you call this a fast and a day acceptable to the Lord? Is not this the fast I choose – to loose the bonds of wickedness, to undo the thongs of the yoke, to let the oppressed go free and to break every yoke? Is it not to share your bread with the hungry and to bring the homeless poor into your house, when you see the naked to cover him and not to hide yourself from your own flesh?'[47] That is the reality of the worship of God, the adoring of his glory in the body of his Son.

But there is a gift of the transfiguration of Jesus. For a moment there is light and radiance and the cult. Worship may be ambiguous but it has its place in christianity. Its place is to keep us from settling for the way things are, to offer us a vision and a dream of the way things could be. We set aside special times and places in order that we may see that all times and all places belong to God, that he has his rights there and is to be worshipped and served there. We come to church in order that we may see that God is gathering his people together from

65

every nation and race and social class. Perhaps the deepest truth is that the point of worship lies in the deliberate entertaining of pointlessness. The point of all prayer is that it be useless, a pouring out of the ointment which might have been sold for much money and given to the poor, a pouring out of time which might have been employed to profit, a playing before God. We are told practically nothing about why God made the world in the Bible. Almost the only suggestion we hear is that he made it for fun, so that the morning stars could sing together and all the sons of God shout for joy. As yet we do that only in gesture, but it is important that we do it. We symbolise things, for man is 'homo symbolicus', the image-maker, the one who in his art and his play finds how to move towards being more himself. Worship does not change the world of itself, but it changes us and we can change the world. It changes us into not being too bothered about ourselves. It changes us as drama and mime make the children growing up in our schools today infinitely more capable of expressing what needs to be expressed than we ever were. In the life of Jesus, too, there are these high moments of gesture – the transfiguration, the anointing at Bethany and, most strikingly of all, his entering into Jerusalem.

Jesus' entry into Jerusalem, meek and riding on an ass, is one of the few scenes, outside the passion itself, which all the gospels dwell on. Jesus and his friends, none of them much more than thirty, out for a sunday afternoon demo with the flower-power of palm branches. Going into Jerusalem when the place was already thick with Temple police and Roman soldiers all set to stamp out any trouble that might flare up at Passover. Burlesqueing the powerful by hailing a distinctly unregal figure as 'King of the Jews'. Some of the serious ones in Jesus' following no doubt found it a bit off: those who wanted him to make a bid at ousting the Romans and freeing the country. It seems clear that some of them were ready for such a coup. At the last supper they produced a couple of swords at least, and people rarely carry swords about their person unless they are prepared to use them. What happened on Palm Sunday, however, is a send-up of that hope, for it was a gesture for power that could not in anybody's wildest imagining capture anything, yet could make people uneasy. Like any successful demo it was a gesture which challenged the way people saw the world and forced the reality of the situation into the open. That is what worship is supposed to do. It should be an occasion when we move out of the world of hard facts and hard faces, the world of what is humanly possible, the world of morality, the world of ought and should and must. We move out of that world into the realm of what is more than humanly possible, which is the world of what, when it happens, will prove the only truly viable way of being human at all.

9

Marriage and Ministry

Jesus Christ is the way in which God humanises the world. He is the sense God makes of our world and its human history. What this may mean we are discovering, in these meditations, by reflecting on the sacramental life of the christian community. In that life believers enact and live out various facets of what it is that God in Christ wants to be for us. He wants to be the one who gives us a new identity, a new heart and soul. He wants to be the forgiveness of our sins. He wants to be the healing of our sickness. He can be all this for us in Christ since Christ is the immediator, the very immediacy, of God and man. Jesus is the man whom God lived and lives. There we see the image of God in which we are made and to which we are called.

For any of us, as for Jesus, humanity is not something we are born with, although the sharing of a common flesh and blood is a necessary prerequisite for becoming human. For us humanity is something we are yet to receive fully. In principle and in principal, in its Head, Christ Jesus, humanity has been lifted up to become tthe humanity of God; there remains, however, the project of the extension of this new humanity in all men. For this incorporation of all mankind into the humanity that is now immediate to God in Christ there is a sacrament. Like all sacraments it expresses, celebrates and effects what it signifies: the making of a new humanity, the immediation of all men in he humanity of God. We call it the church. As the Second Vatican Council pus it, 'By her relationship with Christ, the church is a sacrament or sign of intimate union with God and of the unity of all mankind'.[48] The church is the body of Christ: Christ's way of being in the world, Christ revealing himself in numerous forms and offering himself in numerous ways. But she is so not simply as a sign of a 'datum', of something that already exists, but also as the sacrament of an 'agendum', of a situation yet to be brought about. The whole Christ, the mystical body, is still in process of growing up. St Paul talks about building up the body of Christ until we all attain the condition of Adam fully grown, the measure of the stature of the fulness of Christ. The church is for the increase of the body of mankind as it builds itself up in love. This comes about through a kind of nuclear causality: the whole Christ is a nucleus or exemplary unit which actively draws disordered free elements into its own pattern of organisation, like a chemical or biological nucleus. The pattern of organisation proper to the church we talk about as faith and hope and that specifically christian kind of love, charity.

Of the church as the body of Christ, just as of the eucharistic bread as the body of Christ, it must be said that the whole is in all its parts. When the eucharistic bread is broken, the body of Christ is not divided; when the global community of the church is separated the mystical body of Christ is not divided. Whenever the church meets for the eucharist there is the whole church. The smallest gathering possible would be itself the church since where two or three are gathered together in Christ's name there is Christ and the Holy Spirit and all grace. The gathering of even two people in Christ's name is the church just as intensively as is the great church, the 'catholica', throughout the world. This is especially the case when the two who are gathered together in Christ's name are so for the whole of their lives, accepting together the project of a love like Christ's. The married couple are what the Second Vatican Council calls an 'ecclesia domestica', a domestic or house church. In virtue of a notion going back into patristic times the husband and wife are seen as the fundamental cell of the church. They are, as the Fathers put it, a micro-church and an icon of the church. So fundamental a cell are they, so clearly a microcosm of the whole church and so much her icon that they constitute a sacrament in the most strictly theological sense. That is to say, in their life together they incarnate the church. The give the church a local habitation and a name. They focus the church's being, the church as

69

both a gift and a task, as something already received and something yet to be done.

According to the scriptures this is in any case rooted in nature, in the creation in which we are all made. Adam, Man, in the myth of Genesis, is made androgynous. In his God-induced ecstasy Adam, mankind, is made vis-à-vis himself. In love mankind recovers that unity of one flesh in which and for which Adam is made, as two people are not fused by their union but find self-fulfilment in one another. As Shakespeare says about the phoenix and the turtle, 'Number there in love was slain; either was the other's mine'.[49] Christian marriage gives deeper expression to what human sexuality is in its very roots, for it is the most obvious indicator of the fundamentally communal character of human existence. Sexuality alludes to the fact that people are made for one another, that mankind is called to unity. Christian marriage proclaims that the ultimate unity to which mankind is called is the unity of the new humanity, of the second, wholly gracious, Adam.

This means that the smallest of local churches, the christian married couple, has the task of the 'catholica' itself to go constantly beyond itself. This church in miniature must be the dynamic nucleus of a new society, the exemplary unit which actively draws disordered elements into its own pattern of faith, hope and love. It is not enough for a couple to be a mutual admiration society, with closed doors and interior comfort together, an 'égotisme à deux'. Certainly, some safeguards are necessary: the nucleus must have its own existence in friendship and affection and warmth. Aelred of Rievaulx remarks, in a bold adaptation of words of St John, that 'Where friendship is, there is God'.[50] But the measure of the christian genuineness of this relationship is the measure in which others are drawn into its affection and warmth. Any cell of the church is actively missionary in this sense or it is nothing. In the case of the married this missionary task is first and foremost to the couple's children. The purpose of christian marriage – and a significant strand of catholic tradition says the primary purpose – is for husband and wife to pass over into the wider community of a christian family. It is in this setting that the father can be said, with Augustine, to minister Christ in his home, fulfilling an episcopal office. With the mother, he is a minister of Christ in every department of a common life, washing up together as well as going to Communion together. The fact that marriage has been canonised in the sacramental structure of the church absolutely forbids any departmentalisation of life into parts which concern God and parts which do not. How we worship together in church is not necessarily more important than how we talk to one another or refrain from talking to one another over breakfast. Both are secular and both are religious ways of behaving, since in both we minister to one another the secular man Christ Jesus who is God.

In marriage, then, one person ministers Christ to the other even when one of the married couple is unbelieving, as Paul says in his first Letter to the christians in Corinth. They minister Christ primarily by their self-giving love, contracting the immensities of love in the service of the other. Marriage, according to John Chrysostom, is the sacrament of Eros, of erotic love. It can be so because in this sacrament there prevails the relationship of the one to the other person in his or her totality; hence the erotic element can freely be brought into play as a component of that relationship. One might add that marriage is also and equally the sacrament of friendship, of the love of friends. Because the relationship of each to other prevails, the ordinary values of friendship such as shared interests and mutual concern can be invoked and taken up into the wider reality which is the whole Christ. But marriage becomes a sacrament, properly speaking, in virtue of one thing only, its rooting in the freely accepted passion and death of Jesus Christ. It finds its roots in the Cross through the quality of its love, which is the emptying, 'kenotic' love that was Christ's, the peculiarly christian kind of love which was so odd that a new word had to be found for it – agape, caritas, charity. All relationships in the church are supposed to aspire to the condition of this love which makes marriage the church-in-small. All relationships are to be taken up into this kind of loving which integrates or sublimates, as appropriate, erotic love and the love of friendship.

Since married love involves emptying, sacrifice, sacrificial self-giving like that of Christ, the same language is used for marriage as for the eucharist. Both are said to be the 'vinculum caritatis', the bond of charity. This language is also used about martyrdom. In the greek rite bride and groom are crowned as martyrs at their marriage: they receive the 'stephanosis' (a word made up from Stephen, whose name

71

means 'the Crowned One', the first christian martyr). Throughout the book of Revelation marriage and martyrdom go together, as they do in the subsequent history of the church. Recall St Thomas More talking to his daughter as they watched the monks of the London Charterhouse being led to their martyrdom, 'Lo, dost thou not see, Meg, that these blessed fathers be now as cheerful going to their deaths as bridegrooms to their marriages!'[51] The self-emptying involved means that the married gain a hundredfold, but only at the cost of having that same mind which was also in Christ Jesus, who did not cling to his equality with God but emptied himself and took the form of a slave. This makes marriage another rite of initiation, a crisis of identity with all the accompanying pain of death to the past and of birth to new life which that must mean. 'A man will leave father and mother and will cleave to his wife'.[52] He will have to discover a new identity in being-with, in co-existence. He renounces the domination of another which is so common a part of sexual affirmation. He renounces all narcissistic tendencies, all inclination to seek only his own pleasure and well-being, to use other people in any of the well-nigh infinite variety of ways in which they can be used. That is what theologians in the Middle Ages meant when they talked about the paying of the marriage debt. It is the other who has the claim over our body, that is, over ourself. In committing himself to the other a person gives her the claim on him, to let her humanity be, to humanise her with the true humanity of the second Adam that belongs to the Age to Come.

Of its nature such love cannot be the love of a Don Juan. It is covenant love, a love which is a bond or chain, a love till death do us part or the Lord shall come, as our Baptist brethren put it in their promises. It is a promise for life which makes possible the love of marriage. It is the prospect of permanence that makes any deep love possible. It has to be for better, for worse, for richer, for poorer, in sickness and in health, if Christ is going to be ministered by one person to another. People cannot be truly loved if our love for them depends on their being and continuing lovable, or even continuing sane. If that peculiarly christian love is to be possible between us, each must entrust himself irrevocably to the other, as Christ has entrusted himself to the church. The other is to be loved as Christ loved the church and gave himself up for her. It was while we, the church, were still sinners that Christ died for us. As in marriage so in that other micro-church which is the religious community or the local congregation, we must not allow our love for our brethren to deepen on their being worthy of it. 'What shall separate us from the love of Christ?',[53] asks Paul. What shall separate our brother from our love? Shall his stupidity or his irritating habits or his coldness or his narrowness? The micro-church of the community of a few christians in family and monastery must be as forgiving and accepting as the macro-church of the 'catholica'. It is on that basis that the New Testament speaks about the permanence of marriage. We would be missing its fundamental thrust if we regarded the words of Christ about marriage and divorce as simply a new and more rigorous law replacing the somewhat easier legislation of the Mosaic period. That would be to miss the real novelty in the new and perfect law of freedom which, as St Thomas Aquinas says, *is* the Holy Spirit. To think in legalistic terms about the impossibility of divorce is a mistake. 'In the beginning it was not so',[54] says our Lord. Marriages were never meant to break up, nor religious families to lose some of their brethren. According to the witness of the New Testament there is another way, the way of a forgiving love like that of Christ on the Cross. That is the only way the other person can be truly loved, by being forgiven and lived with until death do us part or the Lord shall come. Let me emphasise that this point has not been taken if we continue to think in terms of a law like that of the Old Testament. For those whose marriages fail or whose commitment to a religious family collapses there must be nothing except understanding and continued care and concern. It takes two to break a marriage or a commitment in religion, and if another person finds that he or she must leave us this says as much about ourselves as about him or her. But equally the sadness remains. It need not be like this. Another possibility is opened up to us in the love we see in Christ on the cross. 'Lord, enlarge my soul', as St Catherine of Siena used to pray so constantly.

The macro-church and the micro-church are both structured communities in which there is a variety of gifts and ministries. The church, both as the 'catholica' and as the 'ecclesia domestica', is not undifferentiated but ordered and patterned. That aspect of its life, too, is said to be sacramental, that very ordering itself. Among the people of God different people have different functions towards each other. In the 'catholica' and in all the communities which image it, people are not only together-in-love but also over-against-one-another-in-service. People are not only together but reciprocal, each other's counterpart. In the face-to-face vision Christ will be the counterpart of his church quite directly. But in this age he has to be represented as such. He is represented as the church's counterpart in the modality of service which is appropriate in a time for building. He is the church's vis-à-vis in those who represent him in serving and building the church.

Our belonging to a structured church involves us, therefore, in service, and in that service in playing Christ to other people. This is what Paul calls being fellow-workers with God and the catholic tradition calls acting 'in persona Christi', in the person of Christ. As vicars of Christ we are commissioned for this task by the one vicar of Christ who is the Holy Spirit. What our ministry is we will discover in a variety of ways, either by explicit commission from another person or by our own understanding of what we are being called to do – an understanding which must be at least tacitly accepted by others. The antiphonal or dialogue pattern of the christian community appears in a variety of ways. Nowadays it is so much more apparent that there is an immense diversity of ways of service in the church: the ordering of the church cannot simply be a matter of clergy over against laity. We all take our turn in leading the singing or ringing the bell which summons people in Christ's name, or reading the lesson which puts the others in the way of being able to hear the Word of God as addressed to them. In the reform of the Roman Liturgy it is clear that the man who presides at the Mass is a hearer with the hearers and a penitent with the penitents. But the variety of ministers has always been there, and ministering during worship is only an expression of a total ministering or representing Christ in the mode of service. The variety of these ministries is there to signify in a clear light the mystery of the church which is the sacrament of unity, a whole in diversity. Paul says that each person should exercise his own particular ministry faithfully and wisely. The Roman Missal says the same: 'Everyone in the eucharistic assembly has the right and the duty to take his own part according to the diversity of orders and functions. Whether minister or layman, everyone

74

should do all that which, and only that which pertains to the gift he has to exercise, so that from the very ordering of the celebration it may appear that the church is constituted in her different orders and ministries'.[55]

This means that often enough we shall be being ministered to, rather than ministering. We are duty bound to let that happen, to let our fellow-christians in our micro-church minister to us. This may well be much more difficult than serving. Letting someone else do a job which you know perfectly well you could have done much better. Letting someone else look after you when you are ill in bed. Letting someone else help you upstairs when you are getting old. If our communities are to image the 'catholica' with fidelity each of us must see that we do not repel the love and service we are offered. Yet at the last both the serving and the being served will go. What will endure is only the being, not the being-for, only the love, not the serving. To that time we must look forward, when signs and sacraments will cease, when there will be no more churches or clergy, when the work of Christ's church will be complete and her Lord will have come.

10

The Passion and Death of Jesus

The demonstration that Jesus and his disciples made as they entered Jerusalem on Palm Sunday did not altogether fail. It did what demos are supposed to do by giving people a glimpse of reality, thus convincing them that they could not bear what they saw. They had to destroy the irritant, this child who was shouting that the emperor had no clothes. They conspired to be rid of him and, in so doing, showed where the power of the world was, and that he had been right all along.

The night in which he was being betrayed the Devil entered into the heart of Judas Iscariot as they sat at table. When the hour came Jesus was sitting at table, his disciples with him. He celebrated the Passover, interpreting the broken 'matzot' as his body and the poured out cup of wine and water as his blood poured out from them. He said, 'Behold, the hand of him who betrays me is with me on the table'.⁵⁶' While he was saying things like this, speaking of broken bodies, spilt blood and betrayal, the inner circle of his disciples, so far from attending to him, carried on a dispute about which of them was to be the greatest. Then he said, 'I tell you solemnly, one of you is to betray me'. They began to ask in turn, 'Is it I?' For a while he would say no more than that it was indeed one of them. It is one of the twelve, 'one who is dipping bread in the same dish with me'. One after another, and among them Judas, said to him, 'Is it I?'⁵⁷ All asked the question, for each knew that the possibility of betrayal lay within him. Judas must have known this like the rest, and like the rest he did not know whether he would be the one who would bring the possibility that they shared into actuality. He did not know whether he would be the one to give expression to the betrayal all were making. A Dominican cardinal, the late Michael Browne, used to say that the only time the apostles acted in collegiality was when they all forsook Jesus and fled! What Judas did was to be the hand and the mouth of them all. As there was a solidarity in vocation. As the study of group dynamics makes clear, we force one another into expressing what there is in us all. By a great variety of subtle pressures we force people into doing things which allow us to say that we are alright. We channel our aggression against the demands of Jesus on to some poor individual; when he can't sustain the demands, we think that all is well with us.

Yet for all of us, the traitors whom Jesus has gathered around his mystic supper, the offer of his love still stands. As the cup of blessing at passover was being poured out Israel used to sing the psalm-verse, 'Pour out your wrath on the heathen, O Lord'.[58] But Jesus says, 'This is my blood poured out for all men'.[59] Even that, for some, can present itself as damning. The offer of that love can be a threat because it demands too much. Not too much hard work and self-sacrifice but too much stepping back, too much accepting, too much letting be. In the Fourth Gospel we approach this from a different angle from the other gospels. John's Gospel does not have the Passover in bread and wine to interpret Jesus' death for us, but a different scene, the Foot-washing at the last supper with the disciples. Jesus, knowing that he was already betrayed in will and desire, rose from supper, laid aside his garments and girded himself with a towel. Then he poured water into a basin, and began to wash the disciples' feet and to wipe them with the towel. He began to do the thing that should have been done already by one or other of them, which they had all forgotten in their excitement and ambition over what they would get out of the kingdom they thought might be coming. He began to do what needed to be done, and what somebody had to do. This was more than Simon could take and he protested, being once again the voice for them all. They could not cope with this kind of Messiah, with a King of the Jews who would demean himself so far as to do what the domestic slave would usually do. They could only cope with a Christ who acted in the terms they thought appropriate. At this stage in the Fourth Gospel this is equivalent to saying that

77

they could only cope with a God who remained God in the way they wanted God to be, and not with a God who behaved as a servant. But, says Jesus to Peter, 'if I do not wash you, you have no part of me'.[60] If you do not allow me to care for you, to do what needs to be done for you, to be a foot-washing God, then you have no part in me. There is no other way of my being man for you and God for you except by washing your feet, with you prepared to have them washed by me. The foot-washing is entirely of a piece with the being baptised. It is only if we can allow things to be done for us that we can have part with Christ. The Alexandrian church father Origen calls on Christ in one of his homilies: 'Jesus, my feet are dirty. Come and slave for me; pour your water into your basin and come and wash my feet. I am overbold, I know, in asking this, but I dread what you threatened when you said, "If I do not wash your feet it means you have no companionship with me". Wash my feet, then, because I do want to have companionship with you'.[61] All the massive systems of morality we build up for ourselves can be ways of keeping God at the distance where he ought to be because there we can cope with him, the lawgiver and judge, rather than where in Jesus he has shown he wants to be for us, washing our feet, answering our need. Faith involves being prepared to have him serve us, to come to us, even as we are betraying him, with his love and forgiveness. It means accepting that in Jesus he has taken us to himself and forgiven us and reconciled us.

In the high-priestly prayer before his death – a prayer which may be a re-working of a primitive eucharistic prayer – Jesus says that he consecrates himself for his disciples' sake. Jesus asks his Father to glorify him so that he may be able to glorify the Father. The glory of Jesus and the Father's glory are not independent, nor even parallel. They are mutually dependent. Jesus, the historical Jesus, the man amongst men, accessible, and observable as we are to one another, was not self-explanatory. Nor is God, the hid divinity, dwelling in light inaccessible, describable in terms which exclude the historical Jesus. The foot-washing Christ translates God for our benefit. And Jesus himself cannot be properly known unless in saying his name you say God. His source, the ground of his being and all being, that which lies beyond everything that is, the meaning of all existence, cannot properly be known unless in saying its name you say the name Jesus. God's glory and the glory of

78

Jesus are one. But it is Jesus who is tangible and audible; it is not that Jesus is like God (who knows what God is like?) but that God is like Jesus. And he is the only God with whom we have to do.

The glory of God and the glory of Jesus are one and the same. That glory, according to the Fourth Gospel, is the church, those of whom Jesus speaks in the high-priestly prayer as 'the ones you gave me out of the world'.[62] These are they who have believed that God sent the Son, that he who sees Jesus sees the Father, that Jesus has no being of his own other than the being in which all creation is grounded. These men, believers, are the glory of Jesus which is the glory of God. They are men fully alive, men truly men, those who live by faith in the Son of God who loved them and gave himself for them in washing their feet and in dying. Such a man, a right and proper man, a righteous man, the true christian, is truly said to live by faith. The faith in question is the faith that the meaning of Jesus is his Father, that the significance of Jesus is the source of all that he is. I am speaking here of the historical Jesus, a man to whom we have access by documents, a man who says that the hour is come when he is to be killed, to be on his own, to be deserted by all his friends and followers, to have no one to depend on, to be frightened in the face of death and to pray to be spared it. That man, in all his historicity and vulnerability, is the meaning of all existence. The believer, seeing and living by that, is someone who does not rely on himself but accounts everything grace and gift. For him the basis of reality is unpredictable and unaccountable, yet utterly reliable. Jesus dies for us, not in us or with us or through us. He is left alone as all forsake him and flee. His life and death are not dependent on us in any way. We are free to depend on him and in him on the source of his life which is the source of all life, the Father. By such dependence, if ever we could depend enough, we would be fully alive, we would be fully the glory of God which is the glory of Jesus Christ.

Jesus dies freely, yet after praying to be freed from the necessity of dying. He is not like Socrates, calmly and serenely drinking the cup of hemlock. He knows the terror of dying and is with us there. He is able to change the meaning of death for us precisely because it meant for him what it means for us, not for the Socratics of this world but for all who are oppressed by death. A few years ago death and the ever-present possibility of sudden death was one of the main motifs in preaching. It was a chief weapon in the battle to persuade people to repent in the approved fashion. Now it has tended to become the great unmentionable in society at large and in religious circles. Death is a fundamental human experience; and more, it has become a part of the authentic humanity we are looking for by being part of the way God lived a human life.

Death in Jesus' teaching is presented as something that comes unexpectedly in rather the way the Kingdom of God comes, like a thief in the night. 'Thou fool, this night shall thy life be required of thee'.[63] What matters is to be ready for it. Jesus has much to say about the ways not to do this. Above all it is the effort to be master of too many things now that ensures our failure to take, welcome and humanise death, to be master of our own dying when it breaks in upon us. 'Fear not, little flock; it is your Father's good pleasure to give you the king-dom'.[64] These words at the Last Supper imply that this desir-able condition cannot be manufactured. Our part is to become able to accept it, to allow God to give us the Kingdom, to permit him to wash our feet. It is possible to make ourselves into the kind of people who cannot accept anything at all. That can easily be our lot if we hang on too much to what we already have, even to what we have from God. Since the dying of Jesus, death functions for christians as a parable of how one should be related to life and to the coming kingdom of God, which will be life in abundance. Death, for those who have heard how Jesus was lifted up in his dying, points to and illuminates life. Not as in some approaches to mortification, where it seems you have to do the best you can to kill yourself now (provided, of course, that you never quite succeed) in order to die better later. The idea that you do the things you least enjoy doing now in order later to be allowed to do the things you want is no part of the christian gospel. What you have to do, to live christianly, is to learn to take life as a gift, as it comes, appreciating it as unmeritable, and altogether free. Supremely, the point where you have to let go in this way is death. 'Father, into your hands I commend my spirit'.[65] We return here to that theme of trust which, as we saw, is the heart of baptismal living. When you come to die you cannot hold on to what you have – families, friends, communities, learning, position, power to do good, all that is best and most desirable as well as what by any reckoning does not matter much. All has to go. Thus physical death becomes the parable of how to live the whole of life, letting go, letting God take over, learning to accept with a definite Yes and Amen. Unless you accept the kingdom of heaven, as a child accepts things, you will not enter it.

Dying, then, must be taken seriously by christians and integrated by them as the most thoroughgoing example of the daily dying and letting go which is the only human way of living. We are to take death seriously; yet death, in Paul's words, has lot its sting. The sting of death is sin, but sin's strength, in Paul's analysis of the matter, resides in the law. It is when you think that life, life now and life eternal, is not a gift (for the kingdom has to be earned and is God's reward for your efforts) that death has a sting. Then it is indeed something to fear: behind it lurks the legal God. But when you have learnt to die daily, letting God be God, and trusting God whose good pleasure it is to give away his Kingdom to you, the sting of death has been drawn for you. Then beyond and behind death is not a magistrate's court with unlimited penal powers but the God and Father of our Lord Jesus Christ, the foot-washing God, the God who is like Jesus and whose glory is the glory of Jesus, which glory we are.

11

The Eucharist

We have been reflecting on the life of Jesus in his church, as
well as in the scriptures, as a way of thinking about what is
involved in being a christian. The church has been defined
classically as 'faith and the sacraments of faith'.[66] The church
is the congregation of those who listen to the word of God in
the hope of Christ's return; while they listen and wait they act
out the meaning of what God is saying to them in many and
varied ways. Faith, the way above all ways in which I am
related to God, the relation that brings life to the just man; the
sacraments of faith, the way faith is ritually enacted and
brought to the fulness of its sevenfold expression. The sacraments are happenings which bring to a point the continuous
reality of the life of the church. They are the concrete expression of the permanent activity of christians. By definition
christians are people related to God in the Christ who is their
new and Spirit-filled life, their forgiveness and health, the one
who loves them, the one who serves them and the one who
represents himself to them in their fellow-believers. But we
may want and need to think not just of the various ways in
which God wants to be for us in Jesus but also of the fact that
he is for us. We may want to celebrate the total mystery in
one, not approaching the mystery of God's love in Christ from
any particular angle but coming at it whole. There is a sacramental way of doing this. We call it the eucharist. In the
eucharist there is everything, so that all the sacraments are
celebrated properly in the context of the eucharist. In the
eucharist there is continual entry into the life of Christ, the

perpetual possibility of a new start, forgiveness and healing, ministry and the love of one for another, the fulness of the Holy Spirit. Great texts of the christian tradition speak of the way we are again and again baptised anew in the eucharistic cup which Jesus fills with the Holy Spirit, with water and with fire. Everything we spell out in celebrating the other sacraments we celebrate in toto in the eucharist, which is the sacrament of sacraments, the sheerest reality of the church itself.

But Jesus is not a stone or a lump of lead. He is a living person, God personally living our humanity, and like any person he is what he is as a result of his past, of his particular history, his biography. Each of us is what he is as a result of our families, our childhood, our youth and all the experiences we have undergone, our activities and passivities. But unlike us Jesus made his own what was done to him as well as what he himself initiated. As one of the Eucharistic Prayers of the Roman Liturgy has it, he went to 'a death he freely accepted'.[67] In accepting that death, so christians profess, he brought forgiveness for the sin of the world. We can come to some understanding of this by contradistinction to the way we experience ourselves. We know ourselves as channels for the sin of the world. We are hurt and we hurt back; we are pecked and we peck; we are put on and we put on other people. But with Jesus this is not the case. We are channels; he was a sponge, taking the sin of the world but not passing it on. Rather, it all stopped there. The sin he took to himself and did not pass on he took with him down into death and left it there. God raised him without it. 'The death he died he died to sin once and for all, the life he lives he lives to God'.[68] He is dead to sin, dead to this present world-order, and living to God in the resurrection, in a different kind of life to which we can go only through death, death by water in the first place in baptism, and then by the continual dying which that death by water sums up and makes meaningful in advance. If we want to celebrate the love of Jesus in its entirety, to affirm Jesus as God's sacrament, we will find ourselves celebrating the life of one who is dead to this present age and alive to a future to which we have to go out in an exodus rather than an ecstasy. We have to go out to him by faith, wherein alone we can find him. He is present to our faith: not because of it but nonetheless to it. So when we celebrate the eucharist we can fairly expect to find it all somewhat ambiguous and to get a sense of

83

vertigo. We celebrate someone who is alive in a new order of things that as yet we can have very little idea of: so much more radically than with the personal existence of each of us he is far from being an object among the many in our world.

The signs themselves, the sacramental symbols, are necessarily ambiguous. They are signs of a real absence as well as a real presence. They are signs that all is not well, but also signs that 'All shall be well, yea all manner of things shall be well'.[69] The signs we are given, be it noted, are bread and wine, not wheat and grapes. They are human manufactures, not unmediated gifts of God from the earth. 'This bread ... which earth has given and human hands have made. This wine ... fruit of the vine and work of human hands'.[70] In being human manufactures they are already ambiguous. 'Generations have trod, have trod', says Hopkins, 'and all is seared with trade; bleared, smeared with toil; and wears man's smudge and shares man's smell'.[71] Think of the conditions in which human hands make bread in our own country and throughout the world. Often it is more unwholesome work than that of enclosed nuns making hosts for the Mass in their convents. Think of the domination, exploitation and pollution of man and nature that goes with bread, all the bitterness of competition and class struggle, all the organised selfishness of tariffs and price-rings, all the wicked oddity of a world distribution that brings plenty to some and malnutrition to others, bringing them to that symbol of poverty which we call the bread line. And the wine too – fruit of the vine and work of human hands, the wine of holidays and weddings, the wine that loosens you up inside and so is such a good symbol of forgiveness, wine which is water and fire in one. This wine is also the bottle, the source of some of the most tragic forms of human degradation: drunkenness, broken homes, sensuality, debt. What Christ bodies himself into is bread and wine like this, and he manages to make sense of it, to humanise it. Nothing human is alien to him. If we bring bread and wine to the Lord's Table, we are implicating ourselves in being prepared to bring to God all that bread and wine mean. We are implicating ourselves in bringing to God, for him to make sense of, all that is broken and unlovely. We are implicating ourselves in the sorrow as well as the joy of the world.

In receiving those gifts back from God transformed into the body and blood of his Word we are implicating ourselves,

84

therefore, in sharing not only what is positive in our lives but what is negative. In communion we are not feeding our faces. We are eating and drinking the gifts of God together. We share with one another what is necessary and prosaic, the day-to-day stuff of our lives; plain, unadorned and with no pretensions we offer it in the gift to one another of the eucharistic Bread. But we also pass on to each other the chalice, and thereby act out our readiness to share the things of the Holy Spirit of God – inspiration, joy, blood and fire, whatever is sweet and intoxicating and passionate in our lives. In the Old Covenant blood was forbidden to man: it was only for God; man's passion needed to be damped down. In the New Covenant he is told to drink the blood of the Son of Man: 'unless you drink the blood of the Son of Man you have no life in you'. Now is the time for our passions and emotions to be not rejected but ordered and made truly our own. Thus in the classical, mediaeval theology of the christian life there are long treatises on the passions. Not to be sufficiently passionate – not to love enough, not to hate enough – is now recognised as a vice, the vice of insensibility. The more passionate a person is the better, because there is all the more psychic energy to be brought into play in his love for God and his brethren, and in his hatred for all that is evil. In sharing the cup we are saying that we are prepared to share that fierce energy and to bring it into play for the good of others.

The bread and wine, then, all this ambiguity and possibility, is set on the Lord's Table. We give thanks over it. We tell a story over it, the characteristically jewish and christian way of praising God, telling God what he has done. Finally we receive back the Gifts in the form of broken Bread and outpoured Wine. We receive them as offered in sacrifice. St Augustine and other Fathers of the church make great play with the nuanced meanings of the expression 'the body of Christ', which refers both to the bread of the eucharist and to the church. These are the two basic forms in which Christ is embodied in the world. The Fathers say that we are there in the paten and in the chalice; when we stretch out our hands to receive the eucharist and answer 'Amen' to the words 'the Body of Christ' we are saying 'Amen' to our own mystery. What we are saying 'Amen' to is bread that has been broken (even if we sometimes disguise this by having individual hosts). The mystery of the church is the mystery of Christ's brokenness, his broken body and outpoured blood, his brokenness and his sacrifice. In saying 'Amen' to that we are saying 'Yes' to the call to become ourselves his broken body. We are committing ourselves to being prepared to be held in the hands of Jesus and to be broken by him, snapped out of what we think we are, where we think we belong, who we think we belong with, who we want to call ourselves. That will involve entrusting ourselves to other people, to people who may take liberties with us, for Jesus is present to us now mediated in other people who play to us the Jesus who holds and who breaks.

The flesh of Jesus is 'for the life of the world'. His body is 'given up for you', for us men and for our salvation. The eucharist, like all the sacraments, is *for* something. It is for the building up of the body of the church and of the family of man. In saying 'Amen' to that we are saying that we too are prepared to be for the church and for the world. At the Last Supper Jesus committed the future and made it part of his own freely-willed history. In accepting the gift of that Supper from him we too are committing the future in advance, saying that we are prepared to be for others, to be given up and broken for them. But the chalice is first of all given to Jesus to drink. The gifts we are given make their demand on us, but only because they first proclaim that they are for us. In their very brokenness and sacrificial character they are for our sakes. The poet of this is George Herbert:

But as pomanders and wood still are good,
Yet being bruised are better scented:
God, to show how far his love could improve
Here as broken is presented.[72]

and again:

Who knows not love, let him assay
And taste that juice which, on the cross, a pike
Did set again abroach; then let him say
If ever he did taste the like.
Love is that liquor sweet and most divine
Which my God feels as blood, but I as wine.[73]

Whenever we eat this bread and drink this cup we proclaim

and placard his dying. Into that self-giving of the Cross we are invited to enter. In the Dominican Use at Mass there is a ritual enactment of this when the crucifixion is being commemorated: the celebrant as he recalls Christ's passion makes himself the image of the Crucified by standing with his arms outstretched, an action which expresses the essence of the Mass far more profoundly than the elevation. This is the gift we have to accept. 'Take', says our Lord, and we reach out for the gift of God with the hands that reveal (and betray) our characters, hands that may disclose the generous man, who is open-handed, or the mean man, who is tight-fisted, and show whether a man is gentle or dominating, distracted and fidgeting or recollected. The Bread of life is given into the right hand, the strong and skilful hand, the hand to work with and write with and fight with, the right hand of fellowship. We take the cup of destiny 'ambabus manibus', 'with both hands' as the Roman Missal directs the celebrant, drinking the cup the Father has given us to drink, which is the chalice of the murdered Jesus of Nazareth.

Christ offers himself in the eucharist as food and drink. In eating and drinking at the eucharistic table we are indicating our readiness to eat and drink, to feed on him, in the multiple ways in which offers himself as our food and drink. The author of 'The Imitation of Christ' talks about the table of the word as well as of the sacrament. Ignatius of Antioch tells us that faith is the flesh, the substance of the christian life. 'Crede et manducasti', 'Believe and you have fed', says Augustine. Basil remarks that the christian eats and drinks the blood of the Word when he shares in his coming and in his teaching. But however we eat the flesh of the Son of man and drink his blood, whether sacramentally in the eucharist, or at the table of his word, or by care for his suffering members, it is always the case that it cannot be done once and for all. We have to go on doing it. The eucharist is the bread and the wine which of itself creates hunger and thirst, the nourishment which feeds desire and longing, longing for the coming of the Kingdom of God.

What we are doing in the eucharist is profoundly involved with that coming. Whenever we eat this bread and drink this cup we placard the death of the Lord 'until he comes'.[74] Until he comes we are trying out for size what it will be like when he comes. He is food for the journey and the end of the journey is not yet. We pray for him to come, and still he comes only in signs, though the signs are his real presence. He comes only in signs, and so in the presence of those signs transformed into him, we tell God that we are still waiting in hope for the coming of our Saviour Jesus Christ. Just at the moment when we are more than ever conscious that he is with us, we say such things as 'Christ will come again' or 'Lord Jesus, come in glory', or we say that we are doing this until he comes in glory. Yet we pretend that the end really is now: we eat together at the banquet God has prepared for us, and drink from the overflowing cup he has mingled and poured out for us. Again and again we wish peace to one another, that peace and unity which belong to the Kingdom where the Lord Jesus lives for ever and ever. It is a prophetic sign, pretending for a while that he has come, roughing out his coming here and now.

We come thereby into a situation where what unites us is the word of God and one loaf and a common cup; this loaf and cup derive their significance from their relation to the death of Jesus to this world and his living to God. In fact they simply are this Jesus dead to sin and alive to God, the one who is God's way of being man. This loaf and cup, which are the way that new and only true humanity is embodied in our world, are what make us a unity. They are what make us the body of Christ here and now, even as in the Kingdom the unity of all mankind will be Christ, the Lamb of the Apocalypse with the marks of slaughter still upon him, the hanged man with the wounds that never healed but were glorified. Here and now we let ourselves be taken into that and live as though that were already so, just as in the liberated zones of occupied territories people now and again live for a while as though the liberation were final. By doing this we are set towards our destiny more fervently. We already feel ourselves at home in what is yet to be and more displaced in what still is. Here and now, with these very unrisen people with all their quirks and foibles and sins, many of them well known enough to me, I pretend that the end of all things which is the meaning of all things has come already. The eucharist is the sacrament of peace and unity between us. There we are, as St Thomas puts it in his hymn, 'com-mensales',[75] people who share a common table. There we are 'com-panions', people who share one 'panis', one bread. The eucharist is 'convivium', a living together, the convivial experience of sitting at the one table and sharing the one bread and living the one life in the Kingdom of God. At the eucharist we are playing at the future. If you want to find out what your real faith in the eucharist is, you should ask yourself not so much what it leads you to say you believe as what it makes you hope for.

But if we play in that way we must be committed to such a futurist style of life outside the sacred time and the sacred place. In the end there will be no sacred times or places. In the Jerusalem that is to come there will be no time,the sun does not go down, moons wax and wane no more. The time and place set apart for the holy as we have them now are there lest we fail to be unsettled and settle for the present order of things. The eucharist is meant to unsettle us, and that in our whole lives. If we take one particular table and cover it with oil and burn incense on its corners and set relics of the saints within it or beneath it, and cover it with fine linen, that is only in order that we may see that every table is something special. If we call one table the Lord's Table, the altar of God, that is only so that we can see that the secular reality of our eating together is meant to be (and in some sense already is) the place where God feeds us with his Son and where we are transformed into him, being broken by the Lord and given to each other. When the Mass is celebrated in our homes there is a sense in which our tables do not then become the Lord's Table but are shown to be that already. Since we celebrate Mass together we are committed to living together all the details of our secular lives eucharistically. That means in fellowship, preferring one another in love. (In the Celtic languages, the ordinary secular word for 'kiss' is derived from 'pax', the liturgical kiss.) It means living from the future, relating to each other as though the absolute future of God had come. We will fail and fall. We will need to be forgiven and to forgive. But we must make a start at living by trusting each other, allowing the other to define me to myself. We can make a beginning at trying not to dominate or use one another, not to hurt and shame one another, not to put the other outside the pale in any way or to use him for our own satisfaction. It may be faltering and hesitating but it can be begun. Inevitably there will be a gap between the way we make eucharist together and the way we live out the details of our lives together. Yet were we not to pretend at the eucharist we could go no further forward. But if we are not continually at the task of trying to narrow that distance we would be better not to make eucharist at all, for then the eucharist only condemns us.

When we thought about what baptism might mean for us we saw that the reality of baptism, adumbrated in water, is baptism of blood. It is the martyr's dying for the name of Jesus of Nazareth, trusting himself to Jesus to make of him what he will, as did the archetypal martyr Stephen. 'Lord Jesus, into your hands I commend my spirit'. The reality of the eucharist also is this same martyrdom, archetypally the martyrdom of blood. The martyrs in the arena of Carthage just before they were killed kissed each other so that they might seal their martyrdom by the solemn token of peace, the same kiss of peace that precedes eucharistic communion.[76] Ignatius of Antioch, as he is taken from Asia Minor to be thrown to the wild beasts in the Roman amphitheatre, speaks of himself in his letters as a pure oblation being brought from east to west. 'I am the wheat of God, and I am to be ground by the teeth of the wild beasts, so as to be found the pure bread of Christ'.[77] He is going to be the real presence of Christ for the world, just as Perpetua told her gaoler that when she suffered in the arena another would be suffering in her. Possibly the finest expression of this truth comes in a letter which a group of christians wrote to various other christian groups about what had become of their old bishop. He was condemned to death by burning and was taken out to execution. When they tied him to the stake he, good liturgist as he was, began to proclaim the eucharistic prayer over himself. He began the prayer of praise and thanksgiving which would transform him into the body of Christ. He raised his eyes to heaven and started, 'Lord God Almighty, Father of your well-beloved Son Jesus Christ, I bless you for having judged me worthy of this day and of this hour, so that I may be accounted among the witnesses (that is, of course, the martyrs) and may take part in the chalice (the eucharistic cup) of your Christ for the resurrection to eternal life in the incorruptibility of the Holy Spirit. May I then be received in your presence today in a sacrifice rich and acceptable.... For this and for all things I praise you, I bless you, I glorify you, through the eternal and heavenly High Priest Jesus Christ, through whom to you with the Holy Spirit be glory now and in the ages to come'.[78] Then the christians whom he had spent his life serving describe what happened next. 'When he had pronounced the Amen and finished his prayer, the executioners lit the fire. A great flame sprang up. And we saw a wonder. The fire formed as it were an arch, and it surrounded the body of the martyr, the witness. And he himself in the midst appeared not like flesh being burned but like bread in the oven'.[79] Polycarp made his dying altogether eucharistic. What is given obscurely in the signs of the eucharist reveals its full reality in martyrdom. In some way we must all be martyrs. As individuals and as communities we must make ourselves into the reality of what we celebrate at Mass. Only thus shall we be sincere in our praying: 'May he make us an everlasting gift to you'.[80] Ultimately our whole existence will be praise and thanksgiving. Our whole life will be singing the praise of the God from whose gift alone mankind is renewed, through Jesus of Nazareth who is God's way of being man.

12

The Resurrection

'The death he died he died to sin once for all. The life he lives he lives to God'. In that dying and rising we share. We are initiated into it sacramentally and we live it out in all the details of our lives. The basic message that we have heard and that we have to pass on, the message which in its first preaching shattered empires and turned the world upside down, is 'God has raised Jesus from the dead'.[81] Jesus of Nazareth whom men killed God has raised, making him Lord and Christ, constituting him Son of God in power.[82] The primitive creed of the church is 'Jesus is Lord': Jesus, the man made in all things like to us, the man who was tempted as we are, who lived through the uncertainty and ambiguity that we live through, this Jesus is Lord. That was the challenge to the system. 'Kyrios Caesar', 'Caesar is Lord', people would shout. And the christians would shout back, 'Kyrios Jesous', 'Jesus is Lord'. 'Clementissime', 'Most merciful', people would shout out to the emperor as he walked through their cities; 'clementissime', christians would say in all confidence to the Father of Jesus at the beginning of the Great Prayer of Thanksgiving. 'Dignum et justum est', 'It is right and fitting', people would yell when the election of a new emperor was announced; 'dignum et justum est', christians would respond to the invitation to give thanks and praise. In the resurrection of Jesus they found what freed them from the world that was founded on power and prestige.

The apostolic preaching was, first of all, that God had raised Jesus from the dead. Secondly, and by extension, it was the telling of stories which hint at what it was like when people encountered this Jesus God had raised. As well as the proclaiming of the fact of the resurrection stories grew up about the appearances of the one who had been raised, stories to suggest the kinds of places where he might be met, and the kinds of situations that were the modes of his presence. Stories designed to hint at how he who came once still comes. Odd and confusing stories, disparate and strange, and perhaps all the more impressive for not being able to be brought into easy harmony one with another. Think how odd the earliest of the gospels is. Three women come early to the grave and find the stone rolled away and a young man sitting there. They are amazed. He gives them a message. 'Do not be amazed: you are looking for Jesus of Nazareth who was crucified. He is risen. He is not here. Look, and see the place where they laid him. But go, tell his disciples and Peter that he is going before you into Galilee; there you will find him'. And then we are told that the women 'went out and fled from the tomb; for trembling and astonishment had come upon them. They said nothing to anyone, for they were afraid'.[83] The way that sentence ends in the original could only be expressed by a line of dots. So abrupt and bizarre did this ending seem even in the first christian generation that other people added endings. Mark gives about a hundred and thirty words to that by which two thousand years of christian history stands or falls. That is his total in describing that without which our faith, according to Paul, is vain and empty. There is no appearance of the risen Jesus, and certainly nothing that could be called comforting or uplifting or triumphant. The witnesses of the first Easter were simply frightened out of their wits. What else could have been the case? They had gone to seek a corpse to anoint and found an empty grave. They had heard a startling message which filled them with religious awe, the 'mysterium tremendum', the 'mystery that makes men shudder'. This is by no means the same as fear of someone or something bigger than yourself that can hurt or humiliate you. It is fear of the altogether unknown, of what cannot be reduced to any previous set of experiences. That is what the original experience of Easter was like, and one thing we must watch is the temptation to domesticate it in the re-telling. One element of being awestruck at the resurrection lies in the unexpectedness of what happened. It might well, it might most easily have been different.

Being a believer in the risen Christ, being a catholic christian, is not something that can justify itself but something to be positively affirmed by us and made our own. It is strange, zany, weird and crazy, this vertiginous experience that drives the women out from the tomb as it will drive the apostles out from the upper room. Just as strange is or should be all baptismal and pentecostal living.

None of the gospel-writers really knows how to end a book properly. This is in the nature of the gospel form. The gospel form is open-ended to our living of it. The risen Jesus in St Mark goes before the disciples into Galilee. That going before is part of our own theme of discipleship. The unsatisfactoriness of the ending is part of the message. 'Master, where do you dwell now?' is one of the questions Mark expects his readers to be asking. And the answer comes: 'I have gone before you into Galilee; there you will see me'. Galilee. Galilee, where the disciples came from in the first place. Galilee, where they had gone about their fishing or their tax-collecting or their guerilla training just two or three years ago, the fishermen and the tax-collectors expecting to be nothing different for the rest of their working lives. Until one morning Jesus had said, 'Come, follow me', and their world had been turned upside down. Galilee of the nations, Gentile territory, the land people looked down on and made fun of, where people spoke with outlandish accents and had strange ideas. Galilee, the world: the world as meaning everywhere, and the world as meaning the secular. For Mark the disciples will see the risen Lord not in the sphere of the holy, in Jerusalem, but in the sphere of the unholy, outside the pale. For Mark the place where we encounter the risen Jesus is Galilee, the saeculum, the secular, the world which God loved, especially the non-respectable bits of it, and there you will see him – as he said! We meet Christ by dirtying our hands in the world, in the affairs of the brother and the neighbour. He is as really present in Galilee, in the world God so loved, as he is in the tabernacle. What differs is not the reality of the presence, as though one were more real than the other, but its mode. To refuse our brother and our neighbour is to refuse a sacrament of Christ. It is to refuse to follow where Christ has gone before. He is always going before. He can never be pinned down in such a way that you know where he is now, in what human needs he is really present to us.

We have two stories in the gospels of appearances of the risen Jesus in Galilee. One is that odd appendix to St John's Gospel: seven of the disciples go fishing, catch nothing and are then told by a stranger to let down the net on the other side of the boat. They do so and haul up a catch of a hundred and fifty-three fishes. For centuries there has been dispute about the meaning of this figure. People point out that a hundred and fifty-three is the number of species of fish in the world according to some ancient sources, although John may have put in the number because he counted them exactly. What is clear, however, is that the scene is an image of the missionary work of the church. What you do when you go to Galilee is to become fishers of men. Going out into the world, the 'saeculum' which God loved, is done in order to bring the world to the risen Jesus. You find Jesus in the process of bringing other people to him.

In the other story of a Galilee appearance, in Matthew, the disciples go north to a mountain Jesus had singled out. There they are told what to do in literal, rather than symbolic and figurative, terms. 'Go, therefore, and make disciples of all nations, baptising them in the name of the Father and of the Son and of the Holy Spirit, teaching them to observe all I have commanded you'.[84] The risen Jesus is found in hearing a command to teach, the high point of all the commands in Matthew's Gospel to go out to preach and heal, to go out footloose, to go out and freely give what one has freely received, to make the word of God not a commodity but a free gift. Meeting Jesus in Galilee is to be given a commission. In resurrection faith there is no seeing without a hearing; no vision without a message. If you are not burdened with a task, your vision is doubtfully christian. Prayer is its own justification, true. Yet if your prayer does not lead you to do something it is doubtfully christian.

In addition to this tradition of appearances in the secular, in Galilee, there is also in the New Testament a tradition of appearances in the holy, in Jerusalem and its environs, the holy city of Zion. This tradition is represented by, for instance, the story of the journey to Emmaus by two former disciples (perhaps a husband and wife) who then worship with some unknown person in a liturgy of the word and a breaking of bread. In that breaking of bread the unknown person reveals who he is and vanishes. Making eucharist is important if we

95

are to find the risen Lord, but it must not be lingered over. The eucharist must not be used as way of tying down the risen Jesus but as a way of learning to find him at all times and in all places. The sacrament of the eucharist and the sacrament of the neighbour belong together. The eucharist as a celebration of the risen Christ should teach us to look for him and find him in our neighbour. When we make another person our neighbour and our brother we can celebrate the finding of Jesus in him by the eucharist we share together, where he is himself present in the feast of love. The mediaeval English author of *Piers Plowman* knew this aspect of the Emmaus story very well:

> For in our likeness our Lord often has been discovered,
> witness in the paschal week, when he walked to Emmaus;
> Cleophas did not recognise Christ before them
> through his poor apparel and pilgrim garments,
> till he blessed and broke the bread they were eating.
> All this was an example to us sinful people
> that we should all be lowly and loving in our speaking,
> and not appear proudly, for we are pilgrims together.[85]

There is but one real presence, through its modalities may differ.

Then there are the stories of the risen Jesus in St John other than the appendix on fishing. These are the Mass stories about the appearance of Jesus on Easter night and the following Sunday night in the Upper Room. A group of christians assembled together, marked off from their normal social milieu, behind locked doors. It is Sunday. Jesus makes himself present to them, saying 'Shalom', 'Peace'. A simple, everyday jewish greeting like our 'Good evening', but one which would never be the same for the apostles again. 'Peace be with you', he says; just as we go on wishing one another the peace of the Lord whenever the Lord makes himself present to us as we gather together on the first day of the week. 'Peace be with you', says the Man with the glorified wounds, as in the Dominican Mass we kiss the chalice before wishing peace, showing in this way the One from whom the peace comes. 'As the Father has sent me, even so I send you'.[86] How often Jesus is referred to as the one who was sent, the man who had a job to do for his Father. Now he says that this job will be that of the apostles and of all subsequent christian generations. There are nowadays two uses of this word 'sent'. There is the ordinary dictionary use of the word, applied to letters carried by the General Post Office and persons deputed on errands and missions. That is the sense of the word which corresponds the Latin 'missio', 'mission', Christians are sent to teach. The other use of the word is the Pop one where people are 'sent', turned on, made high, by music or by drugs or whatever. They undergo interior change, become somehow different. Being consecrated has to do with that sort of change, something deeper than the job, something which makes the job possible. The risen Christ sends the apostles: he gives them a mission and he consecrates them. Jesus sends them by breathing the Holy Spirit on them, the Spirit who turns people on, makes them drunk, driving them out babbling on to the streets. The Holy Spirit is given in order to send people out with the story of Jesus and in order to make them sent with that story's power.

But if we are sent to tell people the gospel we must always be trying to get back to that heart and centre and core of the christian life. It is possible, only too possible, to turn christianity into morality, but as Blake says, 'If christianity were morality, then Socrates was the saviour'.[87] It is possible to get bogged down in trying to lead a good religious life, in struggling against temptations perhaps, or in trying to keep the commandments or say our prayers properly, and miss the one thing necessary, amidst all those necessary and important things. It is possible to lose sight of that thing which comes before all the moral endeavour and the effort to pray, the gospel which makes all those things possible. Christianity is gospel, good news, gift, grace, full, free and overflowing, grace abounding; it is forgiveness, peace and friendship with God, without money and without price. Christianity is the good news that God so loved the world that he gave his only Son, and when the world rejected that way of being human gave him back as a perpetual possibility of a new start. God so loved the world, which lies in a sin that links us all together like runners in a strawberry bed. We all share that situation of sin and in our different ways contribute to it, putting down our own roots here and there and hanging on. God allowed his Son to be made not only flesh but sin. God's Son was involved and tangled up in that plot of human earth. God's presence became altogether what we are. Jesus is so much one with us that you could not pull up that runner without pulling up the whole bed. This is the man whom God has raised. Jesus had stretched out his arms on the cross, letting God be God. That gesture of utter openness gave God his purchase to grip hold of man. God in raising Jesus has raised us too, pulling us all up together in our tangled unity. Judgment has been passed on our humanity: it takes the form of resurrection, the setting free of Jesus into the world God so loved.

If you are prepared to accept this, you can be free. If you believe, you will not fear what the future brings. What is to count as such believing? It will differ from epoch to epoch and from person to person. For the woman with an issue of blood it was no more than reaching out a hand in the right direction, a ritual gesture which embodied more than she could have said. We are told nowadays that the church's sacraments are to be seen as personal encounters. They can be, and ideally they are. But most of the time for most of us they will be, rather, a reaching out of our hand in the right direction. However we take hold of the Easter Lord we know that we shall not be allowed to possess him and pin him down. He comes in the confused, hesitant and here-and-gone words of a man's preaching. He comes in the broken bread and the poured out wine that would decay and turn sour if it were simply left, and when it was decayed and sour would no longer be his real presence. He comes in the oddities and changeableness of other people. But he does come. Still he comes. He comes to make all things new. He comes to breathe on the very dry bones of our churches and communities. He comes that he may breathe on these slain that they may live. He comes, if we are prepared to call to the four winds for the Breath to come, that Breath which is the Spirit of the risen Jesus, of one substance with him who is the Father's way of being man.

13

Epilogue:
the Assumption of Mary and the Goal of the Sacraments

We sometimes find ourselves praying in the Liturgy: 'Send forth your Spirit and you will renew the face of the earth'.[88] Jesus, we say, is the Sender of the Holy Spirit. In raising him from the grave which all men share, God did not so much open the gates of heaven as create heaven. He created his kingdom, the new humanity of the new Adam. 'It does not yet appear what we shall be, but we know that when he who is our life appears we also shall appear with him in glory'.[89] Already we have the pledge and promise of that appearing in the Holy Spirit given us to be the new life of our lives. We have God's down-payment on that future of ours. Already we can act out that future, embodying Jesus who is our destiny. We can embody his dying and rising, his forgiving and healing; we can embody him in the love and service we give each other. We can embody him in his just being himself. These ways in which we embody him or, better, in which he embodies himself with us and through us, are the sacraments. In belonging to a sacramental church, to a church which can be defined as 'faith and the sacraments of faith', we are committing ourselves to the project of embodying what they enact in our total living with one another. To be wholly christian is to be a person who lives the reality which the sacraments represent. The sacraments exist so that Christ who is our life may be embodied more and more in all flesh and blood. They are there so that in re-telling the story of Jesus from one angle after another that story may reach its goal. Celebrating sacraments aright means celebrating them in the conviction that they are only for the time being. It means celebrating them towards that future when they will have passed away and passed into the full embodiment of the Jesus story in the body of a redeemed humanity.

What each of us has done in opting to become or remain a christian is to accept and go on accepting the story of Jesus of Nazareth as the best interpretation of our human living and our human dying. We have entered into that tradition created around the historical person of the rabbi from Nazareth. We have become part of that extended community whose life is continued and deepened by the telling and re-telling of the story of its origins. We tell that story, along with its future, as Sunday by Sunday and even day by day we meet to celebrate the resurrection, which is the whole story in a nutshell. Jesus, a man, a jew, killed, raised, present with us, waiting for us at the end of his history, Jesus gone on ahead. The same story is also told in a more extended fashion, chapter by chapter, through Advent to Whitsun and back to Advent again. We recall the preparation for the coming of Jesus: creation, and the call of Israel. Then the birth, life, death and raising of Jesus. Then the coming of his Spirit, the between-times. Finally, the expectation of his return. The story-tellers themselves, that is, ourselves, spin their story in these between-times, in the space marked out by the lightning flash of the resurrection and the thunderclap of the return. We tell it in time that is punctuated by making eucharist, by that iterative, counting activity in which we mark off the seconds between the lightning and the thunder and find the time charged with expectancy as we count. But as well as spelling out the story in historical sequence we can also spell it out person by person in terms of God and ourselves. It is true that neither God nor mankind can be spoken of except in terms of the other, just as no individual man can be spoken of except in terms of the society which gave him his name and, ultimately, of all men. Yet we can speak of God and man distinctly and distinctively, even though we speak of each as related to the other. Of God himself over against Jesus we can say a little which is little enough. Of the person who is himself the relationship, personally the immediacy of God and man, we can and do say much. If we wish to speak of God in his immediacy to man we speak about Jesus. But just as we can speak about God as related to man but with the human term in brackets, so we can speak of man in relation to God with the divine term in brackets. Jesus does not exhaust God or ḥumanity. He is not only altogether one with his Father: he stands on our side over against his Father. Equally, he is not only altogether one of us: he stands on his Father's side over against us. It is possible to speak of the community which has come into being around the telling of the story of Jesus as being itself over against Jesus. Paul, for example, can speak of that community as the body of Christ. He can also talk about it as the bride of Christ, related to Jesus as to a husband, Jesus' vis-à-vis, his counterpart.

An illuminating way of talking about the church as reciprocal to Jesus, as his vis-à-vis, is to talk about Mary. Mary can function as the best example of what is true for each christian and for the christian community as a whole. She does not stand as an example of humanity over against God. Jesus and only Jesus is that. But she is the example, type and figure of the church over against Jesus. She instantiates the church as reciprocal and antiphonal to Jesus. What we do whenever we celebrate a feast of Mary is to celebrate the human term of the story of Emmanuel, the human side which is not exhausted by Jesus, which is other to him. We celebrate the story of Emmanuel, the history of God-with-us, from our side.

There are special difficulties where it is a question of Mary. 'The Mass and Mary' was once almost a battle-cry as the distinguishing marks of being catholic. The question of Mary can therefore be one where people feel, and rightly, that fundamental matters of loyalty and orthodoxy are at stake. On the other hand, many of us may well feel embarrassed by memories of a time when it seemed that devotion to Mary had cut itself free from sound theology, when fringe devotions were made central and ways of interpreting scripture canonised which would have been thought intolerable in any other area of teaching. We shall only find the true place of Mary in the christian life if we go back to the foundations. We must go back, as the Council did in its chapter on Mary in the 'Constitution on the Church', to the heart of tradition, to scripture and the understanding of scripture in classical theology. One thing that the most classical tradition said and which has now recovered its rightful place, is that Mary is the figure and type of the church, the image and symbol of the new community formed by and around Jesus. If you want to understand what the church is about at the deepest level, think about Mary. If you want to get an idea of what Mary might mean, reflect for a while on the mystery of the church.

The grace or graciousness of God, in christianity's understanding of the matter, has a local habitation and a name. It is not faceless. Its name is the church. It has a local habitation in every man of good will, and a name as multiple as the names of men. It has a local habitation in a girl who lived in Nazareth and it has the name Mary. When we honour her as immaculately conceived, we are just saying that but saying it all the way. Mary is nothing other than the place where the grace of God made its home. Nothing other: she has nothing of her own. There was never a moment when Mary had anything about her to call her own, when she was distanced from God. And this is the way that the church, and each one of us, stands before God. We too are to be wholly and always dependent on the goodness and love of God. The church, whether the 'catholica' or the micro-church, is untrue to itself whenever it calls on power to do its work, when it bullies or browbeats or calls in outside help against those who disagree with it. We must be wholly dependent. We must come back to contemplation, to listening to God's word, being humble before it and letting go. We have nothing as christians that we have not received. Jesus, the person who is one with God and one with us, is wholly God's gift to us in Mary, as he is in that sacrament of sacraments we call the eucharist. 'Take and eat': reach out for the gift of God and take it. 'Take and drink': reach out for the cup that is the new relationship of God and man in the dying and rising of the Lord, let that enter into you and become you. Take it with both hands, as in our Dominican tradition the brethren drink with both hands at table. All is gift, all is grace. It was with that that Mary was filled.

Mary's assumption is her taking into the glory of God not as disembodied spirit but as the whole woman she was. We may think here of that mental picture of the history of salvation entertained by the seer of the Book of Revelation. He sees Israel as a woman, adorned with the sun and the moon and the twelve stars that are Jacob and his wife and children, the chosen people. This woman, Israel, gives birth to the Messiah, doing so in the one woman in that nation who straightforwardly and biologically is his mother, Mary. The child is raised to God's throne; and in that resurrection of Jesus God and man are reconciled. The woman, the church, is nourished in the desert with the manna of the eucharist until the end of time. When we keep the feast of the Assumption, we are celebrating that community, ourselves, what we have been, what we are and what we shall be. We are accepting the invitation to enter fully into the history of salvation as Mary has done. We are invited to take account of the past, as we hear the story of Jesus: we must not despise that natural world of which we form part, that flesh, blood, bones and sinew of man which in Mary already shares in the kingdom of God. We are invited, too, to take account of the past of our race in that constant dialogue we call tradition, for it is a particular woman with the meanings of an ancient culture who has so entered into the life of God. We are invited, finally, to take account of what we are: we must listen to the word of God in the secular world in which we live, and yet live in that world as those not at home there, footloose, unsettled, always looking out for the resurrection which is symbolically enacted in the sacraments and is a bodily reality in Mary.

True devotion to Mary is always bi-focal. It always tends to fuse in one gaze the single historical individual and the household of faith in toto. True devotion to Mary is not to what makes here different ('Blessed is the womb that bore you and the breasts that gave you suck'), but to what makes her the image and perfect realisation of the call of every believer: 'Blessed are those who hear the word of God and do it'.[90]

That is how she can inspire and help us in the following of Christ, in looking at and listening to Jesus in his historical life and his sacramental existence. Perhaps we may leave a final word to a christian monk whose devotion to Mary sprang from her embodying of faith, that faith in which we may find for ourselves God's way to be man. Isaac of Stella, a Cistercian abbot of the Middle Ages, wrote: 'Blessed is the man who never forgets nor lets go of the child Jesus. More blessed still that man who ever meditates on the man Jesus. But most blessed that man who ever contemplates Jesus in the fulness of his stature. And so, my brother, let the Son of God grow in you, for he is formed in you. Let him attain the fulness of his stature in you and from you. May he become to you a great smile and laughter and perfect joy which no man can take from you'.[91]

References

1. Jn 1, 13
2. II Cor. 4, 7
3. Mk. 1, 17
4. Leo the Great, Sermo 74, 2; P.L. 54, 398A)
5. Tertullian, De baptismo 1; P.L. 1, 1306a–1307a
6. Gal 3, 27
7. I have not been able to trace this reference. (Ed.)
8. Hbs 12, 2
9. Lk 1, 28
10. Lk 2, 49
11. ib.
12. Lk 24, 5
13. Acts 2, 33
14. Acts 1, 8
15. Ex. 31, 1–11
16. Rms 8, 26
17. Pentecost Sequence, Veni Sancte Spiritus
18. I Cor. 12, 28
19. Gal 5, 22
20. Second Vatican Council, Decree on the Apostolate of the Laity, 3
21. I Sam. 2, 26; c.f. Lk 2, 52
22. Mk 1, 11
23. Mk 15, 39
24. II Cor. 5, 21
25. Lk 15, 17
26. Jn 20, 20–3
27. Mk. 2, 9
28. Mt 5, 46a; 47b
29. Jane Austen, Pride and Prejudice, ch. 57
30. Mt 6, 12
31. Jn 20, 30
32. Lk 4, 13
33. Lk 22, 28
34. Mt 4, 3
35. Mt 4, 9
36. Rituale Romanum, Ordo ministrandi sacramentum extremae unctionis
37. Jas 5, 14
38. Rms 7, 18–23
39. Joel 2, 25
40. Mt 5, 8
41. The Roman Canon, Memento of the Dead
42. II Cor. 12, 9
43. J. H. Newman, The Dream of Gerontius
44. Benedict, Rule, ch. VII
45. Mk 8, 27
46. Mk 9, 7
47. Isa. 58, 5
48. Second Vatican Council, Dogmatic Constitution on the Church
49. W. Shakespeare, The Phoenix and the Turtle
50. Aelred of Rievaulx, De spirituali amicitia; P.L. 195, 670a
51. W. Roper, Life of More

52. Mt 19, 5
55. Rms 8, 35a
54. Mt 19, 8b
55. General Introduction to the Roman Missal, n.58
56. Lk 22, 21
57. Mk. 14, 18–20b
58. Ps 79, 6
59. Mk 14, 24
60. Jn 13, 8
61. Origen, Homilies on Samuel 1; P. G. 13, 235D – 236 A
62. Jn 17, 6
63. Lk 12, 20
64. Lk 12, 32
65. Lk 23, 46
66. St Thomas Aquinas, In Joan. 19, lect. 5, n.4
67. Novus Ordo Missae, Eucharistic Prayer III
68. Rms 6, 10
69. Julian of Norwich, Revelations of Divine Love, ch. XXVII
70. Novus Ordo Missae, Prayers at the Preparation of the Gifts
71. G. M. Hopkins, God's Grandeur
72. G. Herbert, The Banquet
73. G. Herbert, The Agonie
74. I Cor. 11, 26
75. St Thomas Aquinas, Lauda Sion
76. Passio Sanctarum Perpetuae et Felicitatis 21, H. Musurillo (ed.) Acts of the Christian Martyrs. p. 131
77. Ignatius, Romans 4
78. Martyrdom of Polycarp, XIV
79. ib., XV
80. Novus Ordo Missae, Eucharistic Prayer, III
81. Acts 4, 6
82. Rms 1, 4
83. Mk 16, 6–8
84. Mt 28, 19–20
85. Langland, Piers Plowman, Book XI
86. Jn 20, 21
87. W. Blake, Laocoön Aphorisms
88. Ps 104, 30
89. I Jn 3, 2
90. Lk 11, 27–28
91. Isaac of Stella, Sermo 7; P.L. 194, 1715d